LEO
TOLSTOY

MODERN SPIRITUAL MASTERS
Robert Ellsberg, Series Editor

Already published:

Dietrich Bonhoeffer (edited by Robert Coles)
Simone Weil (edited by Eric O. Springsted)
Henri Nouwen (edited by Robert A. Jonas)
Pierre Teilhard de Chardin (edited by Ursula King)
Anthony de Mello (edited by William Dych, S.J.)
Charles de Foucauld (edited by Robert Ellsberg)
Oscar Romero (by Marie Dennis, Rennie Golden,
  and Scott Wright)
Eberhard Arnold (edited by Johann Christoph Arnold)
Thomas Merton (edited by Christine M. Bochen)
Thich Nhat Hanh (edited by Robert Ellsberg)
Rufus Jones (edited by Kerry Walters)
Mother Teresa (edited by Jean Maalouf)
Edith Stein (edited by John Sullivan, O.C.D.)
John Main (edited by Laurence Freeman)
Mohandas Gandhi (edited by John Dear)
Mother Maria Skobtsova (introduction by Jim Forest)
Evelyn Underhill (edited by Emilie Griffin)
St. Thérèse of Lisieux (edited by Mary Frohlich)
Flannery O'Connor (edited by Robert Ellsberg)
Clarence Jordan (edited by Joyce Hollyday)
G. K. Chesterton (edited by William Griffin)
Alfred Delp, SJ (introduction by Thomas Merton)
Bede Griffiths (edited by Thomas Matus)
Karl Rahner (edited by Philip Endean)
Sadhu Sundar Singh (edited by Charles E. Moore)
Pedro Arrupe (edited by Kevin F. Burke, S.J.)
Romano Guardini (edited by Robert A. Krieg)
Albert Schweitzer (edited by James Brabazon)
Caryll Houselander (edited by Wendy M. Wright)
Brother Roger of Taizé (edited by Marcello Fidanzio)
Dorothee Soelle (edited by Dianne L. Oliver)

MODERN SPIRITUAL MASTERS SERIES

LEO TOLSTOY

Spiritual Writings

Selected with an Introduction by

CHARLES E. MOORE

ORBIS BOOKS

Maryknoll, New York 10545

Founded in 1970, Orbis Books endeavors to publish works that enlighten the mind, nourish the spirit, and challenge the conscience. The publishing arm of the Maryknoll Fathers and Brothers, Orbis seeks to explore the global dimensions of the Christian faith and mission, to invite dialogue with diverse cultures and religious traditions, and to serve the cause of reconciliation and peace. The books published reflect the views of their authors and do not represent the official position of the Maryknoll Society. To learn more about Maryknoll and Orbis Books, please visit our website at www.maryknoll.org.

Library of Congress Cataloging-in-Publication Data

Tolstoy, Leo, graf, 1828-1910.
    [Selections. English. 2006]
    Leo Tolstoy : spiritual writings / selected with an introduction by
Charles E. Moore.
        p.   cm. – (Modern spiritual masters series)
    ISBN-13: 978-1-57075-673-3 (pbk.)
    1. Christianity – Miscellanea. 2. Spirituality. I. Moore, Charles E.,
1956- II. Title. III. Title: Spiritual writings. IV. Series.
BR124.T66 2006
230 – dc22

                                                                2006009457

The only way to be happy is to love, to love self-denyingly,
to love everybody and everything, without any rules;
to throw out from oneself on all sides, like a spider,
an adhesive web of love to catch in it all that comes:
an old woman, a child, a peasant, or a policeman.

— Leo Tolstoy

Contents

Introduction

When Tolstoy was a young boy the dream of flying obsessed him. Surely all he needed to fly was to crouch down and hug his knees and let go. And this he did, at the age of nine, falling from a third-story window, where he was found unconscious by the cook. No bones were broken — all he suffered was a sharp concussion — and when he came to, after eighteen hours, it was as though nothing had happened.

Tolstoy later said that he had jumped not because he really wanted to fly, but to impress others. And for the rest of his life, pretty well everything Tolstoy did, good or bad, impressed others. His attempt at flying was not a passing, childish conceit. He would soon grow up to give expression in a variety of ways to a profound sense that he was destined to transcend the limitations of mere mortals.

By the time of his death in 1910, Tolstoy was known as "the second tsar of Russia." Though he had become the most determined enemy of the state, the most passionate anarchist and critic of the church, he was beloved by all classes and admired throughout the world. Near the end of his life, the Russian bureaucracy reckoned that foreign visitors would want to see only three things in Russia: St. Petersburg, Moscow, and Yasnaya Polyana, Tolstoy's residence. They had good reason to have such sentiments. On his eightieth birthday, Tolstoy received over seventeen thousand telegrams of tribute from all over the world. Altogether, the signatories who greeted Tolstoy numbered about fifty thousand, including Bernard Shaw, Rudyard Kipling, Thomas Hardy, and H. G. Wells.

Tolstoy became world-renowned first and foremost because he was a literary genius. However, among all his other creative abilities, Tolstoy had an uncanny capacity to disturb, unsettle, and upset those around him, while at the same time attracting thousands because of his efforts to live out his unorthodox beliefs. His targets were many: the government, the church, the Westernizing liberals and the literary establishment of his day, the "experts" and intellectuals of all kinds, scientists and theologians. Still, pilgrims from around the world streamed to Yasnaya Polyana.

Isaiah Berlin once stated that "Tolstoy was by nature a fox, but believed in being a hedgehog," referring to the Greek poet Archilochus: "The fox knows many things, but the hedgehog knows one big thing." That "big thing" for Tolstoy was his thirst for perfection, which he later designated as the kingdom of God. His journey toward this goal, oddly enough, was anything but perfect. In fact, it was marked by one extreme twist and turn and inexcusable fall after another. Visionary as he was, Tolstoy's life was full of contradictions, consisting of episodes and attitudes difficult at best, if not impossible, to meld together. From middle life onward, Tolstoy the great novelist became Tolstoy the pacifist, the prophet, the saint. What he had become, however, was anything but conventional; in fact, he was an outright bafflement: how could a novelist's inherited life of privilege be reconciled with a view that "property is theft"? Why did his pursuit of Christian simplicity cause him to be excommunicated from the Orthodox Church? How could his denunciation of philanthropy coincide with his efforts to raise money for the starving masses? How could the prophet of love and peace live in a domestic hell?

Childhood and Youth

Born August 28, 1828, early orphaned, losing his mother before he was two, Tolstoy spent his life in the thin layer of society lying between the Court and the serfs. "In between," as it was, his life would never become "complete," in the sense of being fulfilled. His first eight years were spent at Yasnaya Polyana estate, a large, white-painted, wooden mansion, approached by a lovely avenue of birches and consisting of open, pleasantly undulating farmland leading down to the Voronka River.

Though Tolstoy loved the magical realm of nature, what caught his eye was less his surroundings and more what happened around him. A striking example of this was when his three older brothers were playing in a shady ravine near the edge of a wood. They were whispering about something as five-year-old Leo approached. Nicholas, the oldest, began slowly to announce a marvelous secret that would make all people happy. When the secret was revealed, he said, there would be no more quarreling, no more misfortune, no more sickness, no more anger, and all would become Ant-Brothers. The secret was written on a green stick that had been buried at the edge of the ravine. The very idea of a world free of suffering and malice so impressed Tolstoy that he had himself buried there many years later.

Leo became both bewildered and bothered by how the serfs were treated. Serfs and servants were commonplace at Yasnaya Polyana. Thirty house servants waited on the inhabitants of the Tolstoy estate. Hundreds of other serfs worked in the fields and forests of Yasnaya Polyana. Yet when a neighbor told him how he had punished a serf, because he had eaten meat during a religious fast, by sending him to serve in the army, Tolstoy was utterly mystified — and bothered.

Abnormally kindhearted and sensitive, Tolstoy always seemed to be brooding. There was a reason for this. After he was taken to Moscow at the age of eight, for the purpose of receiving a more thorough education, his father, whom he dearly loved, suddenly died. Not having seen the body, Leo kept stubbornly hoping to meet him on the street. The loss was devastating, and ever after Tolstoy would be deeply pained by the inevitability of death. So much so that this would lead him to devour sweets and sink into lethargy for several days at a time. He would then practice whirling around so as to "catch emptiness unawares." In four years' time Leo would lose three beloved guardians: his father, his grandmother, and his beloved Aunt Alexandra, who had taken him and his brothers in after their father's death. Then Aunt Tatyana, their favorite aunt, was no longer able to care for them.

Though not an outstanding student, Tolstoy pursued a wide variety of ideas with remarkable intensity. At age twelve, he thought deeply about the concept of eternity and the possibility of reincarnation. In order to develop self-discipline and endurance, he would whip his bare back and hold a heavy book at arm's length for as long as five minutes. Self-discipline was one thing; imposed limits, however, were another. Impatient of formal learning, he was bored by mathematical drill. He also balked at memorizing historical dates and at the stern methods of physical punishment of his tutor. These only provoked him into shame and rage. Though the whip was rarely used, it was frequently threatened. Leo was often forced into a dark closet and locked there for hours. It was at this time that the first seeds of religious doubt and murderous imaginings were sown. By the time he was fifteen, he had become an outright skeptic.

When Tolstoy turned eighteen, his mother's vast property, which had been held in trust, could now be divided. Leo received Yasnaya Polyana, with its four thousand acres and 330 serfs. In no time he had marvelous plans for his serfs: school for the children, housing, more nourishing food, better sanitary conditions for all. For the next eighteen months he made a sustained effort to deal generously with the serfs. But whatever he offered them was met with suspicion. They kept on pushing the ancient wooden *sokha*, which barely scratched the surface dust. They not only remained in their mud huts, their children were usually absent from school. All this despite Leo's offer of iron plows, new housing, and free education. The young Tolstoy was completely frustrated.

Somewhat at loose ends, he eventually set out for the University of Kazan. His studies were both undistinguished and curtailed. Repelled at first by the coarse and loose familiarities of student life, he gradually gave way to its noisy and self-conscious carousals, always despising himself for it afterward. He religiously attended the innumerable parties, wanting to dance and flirt but feeling awkward and shy. He dreamed of girls and lusted after them but wouldn't dare to lay hands even on one of his aunt's serf-girls in case she laughed in his face. However, at age sixteen he allowed himself to be dragged to a brothel, where, he recalled much later, he stood beside the prostitute's bed and wept. He was overcome with disgust at the idea of sex without love.

His first-term results at Kazan were so poor that he was forbidden to sit for the end-of-year examination. So after a year and a half, he left the University of Kazan, never taking his degree. In 1849 he went to Moscow, where he stayed long enough to develop a new vice, which in due course would lead him into serious trouble: cards. In St. Petersburg, this new passion led to disaster. On any given night he might lose up to four thousand rubles. His brother Sergei eventually had to bail him out, selling off one of the villages on the Yasnaya Polyana estate — the resident serfs going with it. Tolstoy would not stop gambling until, years later, he gambled away the main part of the old manor house itself.

At this point in his life, Tolstoy had gone wild, recklessly indulging his every passion. He not only gambled hard but was driven to furtive visits to brothels. He also developed a devouring passion for gypsies and their wild music. Several times he was under treatment for gonorrhea, and after his excesses he always fell into moods of despair and self-accusation. His diary is full of self-accusations of every conceivable sin of commission and omission, with day after day, "nothing done." Although among his aristocratic peers there was little unusual about his behavior, he nevertheless had an overpowering sense of guilt.

This was exacerbated by the fact that he strove to live his life according to a clear set of "Rules" — a straight and narrow path of goals, ambitions, duties, and studies, enough to last for years, which were written down in his diary, amended, and almost always broken. Yet he never abandoned hopes of reforming himself. He would just draw up more and more resolutions, even though he saw how ludicrous it was for him to do so.

From Military to Marriage

Tolstoy sensed that his life was heading nowhere fast. To get away from Moscow and to get into the hills, to live free among free people, the Cossack settlers, he joined his brother Nicholas, volunteering on a military expedition in the Caucasus. Unbeknownst to him, though a tiresome, spoiled, rudderless young man of twenty-two, he would return from the Crimea nearly five years later recognized by some of the great literary figures of Russia.

Despite his attempt to turn over a new leaf, while in the military he continued to womanize and recklessly gamble. His diary continued as before: a record of constant lapses into all his favorite sins followed by consequent waves of remorse and shame. But something new began to emerge. His thoughts were now interspersed with reflections about the mysteries of life and religion. He also began to write.

During one of his first battle exchanges, in a surprise attack by enemy hill tribes, Tolstoy managed to keep his composure. Shortly after the incident he was surprised to hear of General Baryatinsky's praise for his calm bearing under fire. He was advised to apply for a commission, which he did. Visions of greatness streamed before Leo's eyes. He began to nurse expanding ambitions: to achieve the Cross of St. George, to become a successful writer, to perfect himself morally, and even

to benefit humankind. With egotistical awe he secretly confessed, "There is something in me that compels me to believe
that I was not born to be like everybody else."

Tolstoy soon realized, however, that military excitement was
rare. He came to despise the boredom and the inane conversation of the officers. His saving grace was his pen. Only writing
made his life interesting. He became more and more convinced
that the thing to do was to cling to his writing: "There is one
thing I love more than goodness: fame. I am so ambitious, and
this craving in me has had so little satisfaction, that if I had to
choose between fame and virtue, I am afraid I would very often
choose the former.... "

During this period he would go on to publish *Childhood*
and *Boyhood* and produce part of *Youth*. He also wrote *The
Raid, The Woodfelling*, and part of *The Cossacks* (which he
was not to finish for another ten years), *Notes of a Billiard
Marker,* and the three inspired Sevastopol sketches, written during the siege. In addition to this, he wrote a large part of
A Landlord's Morning and the greater part of a story called
Christmas Eve, which he never finished. All these works were
largely autobiographical.

What amazed the readers of *Childhood*, his first published
work, were the wonderful freshness and exactness of scenes of
innocence, qualities of radiance and joy which, in the words
of Edward Crankshaw, "sprang not from loose rhapsodizing
but from a precise, matter-of-fact presentation of the physical
aspects of the familiar world as though created for the first
time; a sharp and delicate response to the finest details of tex-
ture, color, odor, gesture, sound, and form."[1] His subsequent
works followed suit. What struck readers and the critics was,
above all, the controlled realism, unstrident, dismissive, low-
keyed description of the human drama. When Tsar Alexander II
read the first of the published Sevastopol sketches, "Sevastopol
in December," he was genuinely moved by the plight of his
soldiers. Consequently, he ordered the story translated into

French and published in a newspaper. The new young empress too wept when she read the plain, open account of the siege, charged with details. No one before Tolstoy had told so clearly of war's brutality.

In 1856, after his wartime experience in the Crimea and at age twenty-eight, Tolstoy moved into the apartment of the famed author Ivan Turgenev. Now of military and literary stature, Tolstoy was introduced to all the key figures of Russia's literary world. Awkward, somewhat aloof, Tolstoy was surprisingly not at all shy to speak his mind, and he could make quite a show of angry violence, attacking everything his writing colleagues loved. He was particularly nasty about Shakespeare and Homer, who, he declared, were worthless phrasemakers. His outbursts were outmatched only by his licentious behavior. He was constantly engaged in drinking bouts, gypsies, card playing into the wee hours of the night, and he would regularly sleep in until 2:00 p.m. He was out of control and knew it. After a visit to one brothel he wrote in his diary: "This is no longer temperament but habitual lechery."

Curiously, in the midst of his carefree, frivolous ways, Tolstoy thought more and more about life and life's purpose. He was particularly absorbed with the meaning of religion and his relation to it. In keeping with his grandiose ideas about life, we read the following entry in his diary, dated March of 1858:

> Yesterday a conversation about divinity and faith suggested to me a great and tremendous idea, to the realization of which I feel capable of dedicating my whole life. This is the idea — the founding of a new religion corresponding to the development of mankind: the religion of Christ, but purged of faith and mystery, a practical religion, not promising future bliss but realizing bliss on earth — I understand that to bring this idea to fulfillment the conscientious labor of generations toward this end will be necessary. One generation will bequeath the idea to the

next, and some day fanaticism or reason will achieve it.
Consciously to contribute to the union of men and religion
is the basic idea I hope will dominate me.

All during this time, Tolstoy was inwardly unsettled. A sort
of volcanic movement was brewing, and he was beside himself. Little did he know that it would be seven years before
he experienced a seismic release. What would erupt would be
his stupendous work, *War and Peace*. But before then, Tolstoy would stream along in an aimless overflow of frustrated
energy, only to be blocked by his own lava-flow. After years of
travel and experimental activities of various kinds, he and all
those who admired his literary talents were to despair about his
writing future.

By 1860, Tolstoy felt he had dried up as an author. He had
become disgusted with high society and with himself and began
to turn his energies to teaching in a village school near Yasnaya
Polyana. This time he persuaded his serfs to send their children
to be taught by himself. He had tried something like this two
years earlier, but the peasant children never felt free enough to
stay away from working the fields. Now with emancipation in
the air, many of his serfs realized that their master's free school
might actually benefit their children. Twenty-two children were
enrolled, and Tolstoy began to carry out his unique educational
principles.

As if he were reinventing pedagogy altogether, the children
were not to be taught, but to teach themselves. His goals were
few but clear: establish a simple, easy, and independent relationship between master and pupil; cultivate mutual affection and
trust; free class lessons from constraint and learning by rote;
and transform the school into a kind of family. In his school,
"No one brings anything with him, neither books nor copy-
books. No homework is set them.... They are not obliged to
remember any lesson, nor any of yesterday's work. They are not
tormented by the thought of the impending lesson. They bring

only themselves, their receptive nature, and an assurance that it will be as jolly in school today as it was yesterday." External disorder, in his opinion, was actually useful and necessary, however strange and inconvenient it may seem to the teacher. One only needed to wait awhile and the disorder would eventually calm down of itself. This, he claimed, is exactly what he experienced. In the end, Tolstoy condemned all formal education without exception.

Tolstoy's work with children would become a saving grace. It not only focused his energies, but turned him toward a constructive endeavor. It would also prepare him for a family life of his own. Two years later he became engaged and married to Sonya Bers. Sonya was an eighteen-year-old girl who was graceful, dark-haired, given to romantic melancholy, but with an alluring smile. She also possessed tenacity, energy, intelligence, and a capacity for family affection. Despite her own capabilities, she was young and intimidated by her new fiancé. Whether or not the marriage was doomed from the start one cannot say. However, it would end in spectacular disaster — a disaster that was long prepared.

At first, harmony and joy prevailed between them: "I didn't know it was possible to be so much in love and so happy," Tolstoy would write. But there were quarrels, in part because Sonya, after reading Leo's diary, which he gave to her the day before their wedding, knew that Aksinya, a local peasant who was his most recent mistress, still lived on the estate. Besides, moving to Yasnaya Polyana was extremely frightening for a young Europeanized city girl. As A. N. Wilson points out, "There was nobody there who could possibly become her friend, no substitute for her sisters, for instance, nor for the innumerable, polite, harmless, jolly people who streamed in and out of her mother's Moscow drawing room."[2]

Still, Sonya was committed to seeing that the Tolstoy style of life was one to be envied. Their house was enlarged and remodeled, with plenty of room for an endless stream of guests and visitors. Extra servants in crimson waistcoats appeared among the regular retainers. In the first ten years of marriage, Sonya would give birth to six children. In all, they had thirteen. It would be a happy period. Along with guests, jokes and comic verse would be read with glee at the large dinner table. Piano duets were played, and the family would pick mushrooms, go sleigh-riding, put on plays, read and organize costume balls together. The children took turns at playing chess with their father, and on warm evenings Tolstoy would take them out to examine the night sky. Frequently the family visited neighboring estates, where they would indulge in fabulous dinners, dancing, and music.

In general, the children had a firm bond with their father. They loved and admired him, and found him the jolliest of companions. They loved the way he took an interest in them and would do things with them. No guessing game could outwit him. And he was always up to some sort of prank or game, whether it was the basket game when one of them would be put in a laundry basket with the lid on and carried through the house and made to guess which room he or she was in; or, at a signal, getting *en masse* under the table so that the dining-room seemed completely empty when their mother came in for the meal.

One result of getting married was that Tolstoy had to abandon his educational work. Sonya was very exacting and demanded that he financially provide for her and for their family. And as fate would have it, what had been brewing beneath the surface for some years finally erupted in what some consider the greatest novel ever written. Together and for the next six years, Sonya furiously plunged herself into the self-appointed task of protecting her husband from the outer world, and copying and recopying what would later be titled *War and Peace*. All the while, Tolstoy pored over volume after volume of Russian history, revising almost everything that poured forth from his pen. When the proofs came back, Tolstoy made yet more corrections and additions, in a crabbed, illegible hand that blackened the page. Sonya alone could decipher his scribbles — truly alone. Even Tolstoy, at times, could not make out what he had written. By the time the book was finished, in 1869, Sonya had written out the equivalent of seven complete copies of the whole book, which was over a thousand pages long. It is improbable that, without his wife's help and guidance, the work would ever have been finished.

Upon its completion, Tolstoy was in no mood for either novel-writing or novel-reading. Although publishers flooded him with offers of ten thousand rubles in advance for a new book, and five hundred for every page, he took no notice. He despised journalists, disliked periodicals, and hated the press. He also despised life. He had completed a masterpiece, but it left him inwardly exhausted — empty and void. In *War and Peace* Tolstoy faced the harsh and terrible fact of mortality. Generation after generation lives and dies — to what purpose? Leaving what behind? At this juncture, Tolstoy did not see this life as a preparation for another, and thus he made sure to seal all possible exits for the living. What else is there? *War and Peace* ends in a series of unanswerable questions: What forces move the nations? Why do things happen? Why are we here? With Schopenhauer, Tolstoy seriously wondered, "What is the point of anything?"

The fatalism that characterized *War and Peace* had gotten a grip on his soul. In actual fact, the novel had become a vain attempt to keep at bay the fundamental questions about life's meaning and death, which at bottom had plagued him for years. Sonya was fully aware that some dreadful obsession held her husband. "His lack of direction is a great trial to him," she lamented in her diary. "Sometimes he thinks he is losing his mind, and his fear of insanity is so intense that I am terrified when he tells me about it afterward."

Despite his inward alienation, or perhaps, because of it, Tolstoy, at his wife's persistence, managed to produce yet another great novel, *Anna Karenina*. How he managed to do this is itself mystifying. He did not want to write another book. And when *Anna Karenina* was finished, he thought poorly of it. He actually never liked it, and according to his son Ilya, always wanted to disown it. The entire novel was written under the shadow of death. Of the 239 chapters, he gave a title to only one: the twentieth chapter of the Fifth Part, which he called, "Death." After *Anna Karenina* there would be no more great novels.

The Search for Truth

To assuage his conscience, and perhaps to numb his angst, Tolstoy reopened a school at Yasnaya Polyana. In 1871, he and his wife happily worked on an ABC book for children. In it he tells stories about his dogs, Milton and Bulka, and retells old Indian or Arabic legends, Bible stories, and folk tales. Tolstoy even makes up stories of his own, some of which, such as *A Prisoner in the Caucasus,* are great works of art, elegant, concisely told, and completely simple.

Despite success on all fronts, Tolstoy unraveled. He was plagued with suicidal thoughts, even to the point of hiding a rope, lest in a surge of sudden despair he take his own life. He consumed philosophy texts of every school of thought — Schopenhauer and Plato, Kant and Pascal — hoping to find some explanation to the meaning of life. But neither the philosophers nor the sciences, not to mention his own contemporaries, helped him find what he was looking for. The "wise men" of history were clear and exact, but only where they did not deal with the real questions of life!

In observing the responses of his own circle to the problem of existence, it came to him that there were four possible paths out of his dilemma. The first was blithe ignorance. Not knowing that life is hopeless would mean not caring. It was too late for that. The second was the way of pleasure. Just eat, drink, and be merry, as Solomon suggested. Most people followed this path, as Tolstoy himself did; but Tolstoy could no longer do so. The third escape was strong and energetic. If life is evil, then it must be destroyed. Buddha was right in insisting that we must free ourselves from life. Suicide? Could he come to that? Perhaps. Yet he found himself feebly following the fourth way — to his mind, the despicable path of weakness. Clinging to his life like a coward, he was almost certain that it had no purpose, nor any meaning that could not be destroyed by death. Tolstoy was stymied, frozen in the midair of a meaningless existence, awaiting annihilation.

Then it occurred to him to look beyond his own circle. The curious thing was that the masses of people, the poor and the oppressed and the peasants, lived life on the instinctive sense that it did have purpose. Their faith in God, their simple labor and dedication propelled them to live. And then it dawned on him: he too only lived at those times when he believed in God. "I do not live when I lose belief in God. I live, really live, only when I feel him and seek him." "What more do you seek?" cried a voice within him. "This is he. He is that without which one cannot live. To know God and to live is the same thing. God is life. Live seeking God, then you will not live without God." And then all within him and around him lit up; the light never left him.

To nurture his newfound faith, Tolstoy became a regular attendant at the little village church at Yasnaya Polyana. He strove to enter into the spirit of the peasants and to overlook the contradictions, obscurities, and superstitions of their cult. But finally something turned him away from the church. It was not a matter of form or theory, but a purely ethical matter, which shocked his essentially practical mind. It was in the year of 1878, and the great Russo-Turkish war had broken out. The Holy Synod ordered prayers to be said in the churches for the success of the Russian armies, and when Tolstoy heard the lips of the priest, who had so often read the Gospel injunction to love your enemies and do good to those who despitefully use you, utter supplications in the name of Jesus to the Almighty that he might destroy the Turks with sword and bombshell, or words to that effect, his soul revolted at the blasphemy, and he walked away from the church for good.

Right from the start, Tolstoy understood God in terms of life. To seek God was to sacrifice oneself for the sake of others. As early as the fifties, when writing *The Cossacks*, Tolstoy already sensed the truth of this. The character Olenine wonders why he had never been happy, and he runs over his life in his mind and its selfishness fills him with disgust. Suddenly, the light burst upon him. "Happiness," he cries, "happiness consists in living for others, that is clear. Man aspires to happiness; therefore it is a proper desire. If he tries to get it in a selfish way, in seeking wealth, glory, love, he may not succeed, and his wishes remain unsatisfied. Then it must be selfish desires that are wrong, and not the wish to be happy. What are the dreams that may be realized irrespective of our outward circumstances? Only love and self-sacrifice." He jumps up, rejoicing in his discovery, and seeks impatiently for some one to love, to do good to, to sacrifice himself for. And when he returns to the village he insists upon presenting his horse to a young Cossack who had been his rival in the affections of one of the village maidens.

Like Olenine, Tolstoy's conversion led to numerous outward and visible signs of sacrifice. Worldly goods and all the surface attractions began to appear to him as shackles and eventually became a cross he found hard to bear. The burden was so heavy at times that he sought to slough them off, to break with his entire past, to reject the family life he had dreamed of in his youth, and finally to give up all the wealth he had acquired, renouncing his property and giving up the profits from the sales of his books.

Tolstoy thus took concrete steps to implement his convictions. For example, he would take the family tutor to walk past the kitchen with him to guard him against temptation, as he found Domna, the cook, far too attractive. Though early on he allowed himself alcohol, tobacco, and meat — all of which he would in the course of time eschew — he took to wearing peasant costume and undertook menial tasks that might have been performed better by artisans. He made his own boots, for instance, and went about in a sheepskin coat and a cap like a peasant. He eventually gave up hunting and became a vegetarian. He also gave up the title of Count, as well as other titles, and frequently farmed in the fields with the peasants he admired. He even tried to give up sexual relations with his wife, but couldn't manage. Everyone was horrified by his behavior, especially when he insisted on dealing with his own chamber pot.

Tolstoy often urged his children to join in these projects, but their enthusiasm usually did not equal his. More often, they accused him of becoming gloomy and disagreeable. Sonya especially resented her husband's religious efforts. She was aghast at his repudiation of the Orthodox Church, which according to him was a partner of the state, "cheating and fleecing the people." In 1879 Sonya wrote to her sister: "Leo reads and thinks until it gives him a headache. And all in order to prove that the church does not accord with the Gospels.... My only hope is that he will soon get over it, and it will pass like a disease."[3]

Little did Sonya know that it was far from being a passing phase, and that her husband was embarked on a religious warpath that would throw her and him into one debilitating battle after another. Eventually, his whole household was torn by strife.

The Widening Divide

For the next thirty years Tolstoy shunned his literary career and devoted himself to writing serious religious tracts. His books such as *My Confession*, *The Four Gospels*, *A Criticism of Dogmatic Theology*, *What I Believe*, *What Then Must We Do?* were all written without expectation of immediate publication, and none of them were officially published first in Russia. Nevertheless, unofficial copies from abroad, and lithographed ones at home, spread throughout the country with rapidity and were read by an enormous audience.

As long as Tolstoy's work was literary, Sonya took a lively interest in it. But his philosophical and theological and social-critical labors were far too abstract for her and left her indifferent and hostile. Sonya's animosity to her husband's religious ideas only intensified. She nagged and harried him. She objected to his work, to his followers, and even to the way he dressed. Sometimes she definitely seemed emotionally unstable. Swollen with resentment, she would sometimes fling herself out-of-doors in freezing weather and hide in a ditch while the entire household searched for her.

Tolstoy felt especially alone during this period; but in their respective diaries both felt misunderstood, abandoned. Sonya felt useless, but Tolstoy felt spurned by all those around him, as he could no longer live a life of carefree idleness, especially when living only a stone's throw from people who were dying of poverty. "At home," he writes in his diary, "a big dinner with champagne. Tania in a smart dress: each child wearing a sash worth five rubles. While we dined the carriage had already left for the picnic, amongst peasant carts which were bringing back people made ill with overwork." And though he saw quite clearly that his wife was incapable of understanding the path he was on, he was determined to turn his back on his superfluous life and create a new one more in conformity with his beliefs.

By 1884 he had become a vegetarian. At table, there were outbursts of rage if the food was too elaborate. He wandered around the village, inspiring a mixture of respect, gratitude, confusion, and embarrassment as he fraternized with his peasant friends. On one day he would help an old woman to rebuild her hut. On another, he would go and chop wood for some poor family. But when he returned home in the evening Sonya,

tired and hot, and in her confinement, taunted him with inconsistency. How could he let his own farm run down in the name
of Christian love?

Tolstoy did not know what course to follow. He frequently
declared that it would be better for him to leave home and
become a beggar wandering through the land, however painful
and uncomfortable that may be, than endure living the way he
did at home, where all those aspects of his being which he considered the most important were utterly unacceptable. "I cannot
find a way of treating my wife so as not to hurt her feelings and
not give in to her," he wrote in his diary.

Sonya was particularly anxious about their finances and the
future of his literary works. She worked hard to bring out a
new edition of his works, and argued bitterly with Chertkov,
Tolstoy's assistant, who wanted some of them for *The Inter-
mediary*. She fought desperately for the funds she deemed
necessary to sustain the family's standard of living — a standard
that, though a violation of Tolstoy's beliefs, she considered both
proper and essential. Since he had abandoned any responsibility for the *Collected Works*, she simply felt compelled to take
on the role of breadwinner for their large family.

What Then Must We Do?

Though he and Sonya quarreled frequently, family strife did
not prevent Tolstoy from actively pursuing and living out the
implications of his faith. As a Russian landowner at a period
when serfs had only just gained their freedom, Tolstoy was
hardly blind to the disparity between the rich and the poor;
but it was not until Sonya pressured him into buying a house
in Moscow and after seeing the slums that he realized how bad
social conditions were — and he was appalled.

He went visiting prisons and houses of detention, sat in on
all the cases being tried by the district courts and justices of
the peace, and watched desperate young men being recruited

into the army. It was as though he were deliberately going everywhere looking for places where he could see human suffering and violence being done to people. And as he rummaged through the city, he began to hand out large sums of money right and left, which, naturally, terrified Sonya. But he just dug in his heels all the more, often quoting the Gospel: "Give to them that ask you!" He even volunteered as an official to help with the 1882 municipal census. It was here that he observed the moral deterioration that overtook those who had slipped down into society's slums. He was shattered by the experience and came to the realization that Moscow "was nothing but a vast open sewer, a stinking cesspool."

As Tolstoy was out mixing with the poorest, Sonya would spend her days paying or receiving visits. On their "at-home day" she, with the children, would sit around and wait to see who would turn up. Then tea, fancy cakes, sandwiches were served, all of which were consumed with gusto. On the other days they were entertained in like fashion.

Tolstoy could no longer cope with the contradiction between his life and what he saw. Against his wife's wishes, he left Moscow to return to Yasnaya Polyana. It was then he poured everything out. In his book *What Then Must We Do?* Tolstoy describes the plight of the urban poor, and few descriptions of urban poverty have bettered this. It all starts when he sees a ragged peasant, swollen with dropsy, being arrested for begging. His shock at the sight takes him to doss houses around the Khitrov market. The first fourteen chapters of the book contain human sketches that, in the words of A. N. Wilson, "are every bit as good as anything in his novels, animated by a sense of violent moral outrage about the divisions between rich and poor."[4]

In answer to the question of the book's title, Tolstoy came to a simple conclusion: repent, live self-sufficiently, engage in manual labor, live and eat simply. The privileged classes must no longer expect to be fed, clothed, and waited upon by others;

they must "get off the backs of the poor" and obey the basic law of life. Unless this occurs, there was no doubt in Tolstoy's mind what would happen. "Only one thing is left for those who do not wish to change their way of life, and that is to hope that 'things will last my time' — after that let happen what may. That is what the blind crowd of the rich is doing, but the danger is ever growing and the terrible catastrophe draws near." And, as we know now, it did come some twenty years later.

In 1891, Tolstoy finally managed to officially renounce the rights to virtually all his works published after 1881, allowing his earlier works to financially benefit the family. He soon gave away all his property (valued at 580,000 rubles) in ten shares, to Sonya and their nine living children.

By now, Tolstoy's life followed a kind of "prophetic routine," combining work, writing, and taking up various social causes. As soon as he woke up he went out into the fields and woods to "say his prayers." People perpetually waited for him, lying in wait inside the house or preparing to ambush him around a bend in a path: pilgrims, poor people, peasants. Three post offices delivered a daily mound of books, letters, newspapers, magazines that came from all over the world. After satisfying his visitors and correspondents, he settled down to write. He would then spend his evenings with the family and any other visitors. Before going to bed he would bring his correspondence and diary up to date.

All this was set against the backdrop of the famine of 1891, affecting the drought-scorched provinces of central Russia. While the government callously ignored the disaster, thousands of peasants were slowly dying of starvation. Against Sonya's wishes, Tolstoy left for a tour of the drought areas, taking with him his oldest daughters, Tanya and Masha. Everywhere the large sad eyes of listless, bony children stared at them over swollen, empty bellies. Gaunt peasant mothers deprived themselves of their little food in order to keep the young alive. Many had already died. In response he worked in the provinces for months. Using money reluctantly sent by Sonya, they bought firewood, set up crude bakeries, and organized free kitchens. Within three months time, hundreds of kitchens had been organized, feeding ten thousand people daily.

Tolstoy, now sixty-three years old, supervised volunteers and the distribution of supplies by day on horseback. By night, he composed a torrent of heartrending articles, pleading with Russia to help her perishing people. Tolstoy blamed the nobility for the drastic food shortage. The articles were naturally censored in Russia, but were still published abroad. At last donations poured in from all over the world. Volunteers followed. Even Sonya was won over; she soon collected thirteen thousand rubles for the emergency. Tolstoy successfully brought relief to the peasants, feeding as many as sixteen thousand people daily. In 1893, the rains returned. Crops prospered. With the people saved, Tolstoy came home.

Paradoxically, despite the success of his efforts at relieving the misery of the masses, Tolstoy was a relentless critic of philanthropy, without which he could have done very little for the famished stricken peasants. Ten years earlier, in 1881, while in Moscow, he happened to meet the peasant secretary and religious reformer Soutaieff and explained to him his plans for the care of the aged and orphans and for putting an end to all the misery in the city. Tolstoy asked him what he thought of the scheme. "That's all nonsense," was the answer. "Are there not a million hearths in Russia?" he asked. "Let us work with them, and have them eat at our tables and hear good words from us; that would be true almsgiving. All the rest is absurdity."[5]

Tolstoy came to believe that far from uniting people in bonds of affection, nothing separates them so surely as money given and taken in the way of ordinary charity. "If a horseman sees that his horse is tired out, he must not remain seated on its back and hold up its head, but simply get off," he used to say, condemning all the charities of the well-fed people who sit on the

back of the working class, continue to enjoy all the benefits of
their privileged position, and merely give from their superfluity.
In fact, catchwords like Fatherland, Freedom, the State, were all
nothing but a ploy to protect the property that does not really
belong to those who have it. The state's role was ultimately to
shield all the injustice of present-day society; it was thus a fic-
tion, invented only to protect a many-meshed system of force,
with laws, prosecuting attorneys, prisons, judges, policemen,
armies.

During the following years, several religious groups appealed
to Tolstoy for help against the atrocities of government authority. The best-known group, the Dukhobors, was a sect of
un-Orthodox Christians founded on the belief that military service and bearing arms was a sin. Government officials and the
hierarchy of the state-controlled Orthodox Church hated and
feared this unusual Christian sect whose young men refused to
serve in the army. Drastic action was finally taken. During a
gathering in which weapons were burned, while praying and
singing psalms, the Cossacks arrived with whips and began to
flog the Dukhobors mercilessly. The governor himself helped
to flog them. Thousands of helpless pacifists were driven away
into the mountains, where a great many died. Their homes were
burned, their lands confiscated, and their leader banished.

Tolstoy wept when he heard of this savagery. He then began
a campaign to try to relieve this sect of seven thousand believers. He sent a vitriolic description of the outrageous mistreat-
ment of the Dukhobors to London, where it was printed as *The
Persecution of the Christians in Russia.* Copies went to every
important member of the government, including Nicholas II.
Instead of help, there came reprisal. Two of Tolstoy's devoted
followers, Chertkov and Biryukov, were exiled. Sonya was
afraid that her own family might be deported, but Tolstoy
continued his petitions to the tsar. Eventually, the government
permitted the Dukhobors to settle on uncleared land in Canada.
Tolstoy then collected an enormous sum to help transport them.

All the profits of his story *Resurrection* went to the emigration expenses of the Dukhobor refugees.

Tolstoy would take up many others causes on others' behalf. When Molokhan children from Samara were seized and forced into orphanages, on the grounds that they should be trained according to the Orthodox Church, he again wrote to Nicholas II. After numerous failed appeals, the children were finally returned. In 1902, Tolstoy was horrified to hear of a savage massacre of Jews in Kishinev. He wrote bitterly to the governor of Kishinev.

All this activity was the consistent working out of his belief in nonviolence, a belief he came to on the basis of Jesus' Sermon on the Mount. For Tolstoy, only a fool would attempt to stop the pendulum when it swings to the right by pushing it as violently to the left, and yet this is the chief object of most of our legislation and military action. Jesus always looked deeper. The great sin was not killing but anger against a brother. The problem was not how to prevent murder but how to eradicate anger and fear and hatred from the breast of man. This, for Tolstoy, was the key in overcoming every social problem. And he was convinced that the truth of nonresistance would prevail. "People long ago were unable to see that indulgences, inquisitions, slavery, and torture were incompatible with Christianity. But a time came when they saw it as comprehensible. And a time will come when people will see Christian faith is incompatible with war service and service to the government in general. Government is violence, Christ's way is meekness, nonresistance, love. It is that simple."

Last Battles

If only Tolstoy's life had been as simple as he envisioned the Gospel. But it was not. Sonya and he would grow further and further apart. First, the death of their youngest son, Vanya, completely shattered Sonya's existence. Then Sonya's infatuation with her piano tutor drove Tolstoy to fits of jealousy and rage. And then there was the question of the will, which Tolstoy managed to change several times, aggravating Sonya's already existing mistrust. Finally there was the gaping divide between Tolstoy's convictions and the lavish lifestyle of his home, which, in the end, became for him unbearable.

None of this was helped by the fact that Tolstoy had now become an international celebrity. He was in warm correspondence with Mahatma Gandhi in India and George Bernard Shaw in England. When William Jennings Bryan visited Yasnaya Polyana, he gave up an audience with the tsar in order to spend an extra day in conversation with Tolstoy. In 1907 Thomas Edison sent him a Dictaphone.

His notoriety unnerved government officials. Finally, when his book *Resurrection*, in part a shocking indictment of the Orthodox Church and the state that supported it, came out, the authorities decided that Tolstoy had gone too far. Fearing that either exiling or imprisoning Tolstoy might set off a popular revolt, the church excommunicated him in 1901. Yet on the day the edict was pronounced, Tolstoy was in Moscow, and as he turned into Lubyanskaya Square, he saw a crowd of several thousand. "There he is!" called out a voice and quoted with heavy irony from the deed of excommunication, "The Devil in human form!" Cheers broke out. "Hurrah, Leo Nikolayevich! Greetings! Hail to the great man!" A flood of letters, flowers, telegrams, and expressions of sympathy poured in as a result of the excommunication.

Fame was not Tolstoy's forte. But by now Tolstoyan colonies, based on the duty of manual labor, or "bread labor," were popping up everywhere. Tolstoy himself never took part in any of these colonies, and in fact disliked them. None of them were successful, except Gandhi's "Tolstoy Settlement" in the Transvaal. Their deficiency lay in the fact that they limited themselves to imitating Tolstoy in externals without grasping the deeper meaning of his ideas. Tatyana, Tolstoy's daughter, recalls her father's attitude toward many of his would-be disciples:

One day, among the group surrounding my father, I noticed a strange young man in a Russian smock, baggy trousers, and top-boots. "Who is that?" I asked my father. Papa leaned toward me, put his hand in front of his mouth, and whispered in my ear, "He is a young member of what is to me the world's most strange and incomprehensible sect: The Tolstoyans."[6]

Aside from official edicts, for those who were skeptical of Tolstoy's ideas, and of Tolstoy himself, there was no end of accusation. Though technically having renounced his possessions, he still lived in a style which most Russians would have regarded as luxurious, and his simple vegetarian meals were served to him by a lackey wearing white gloves. One caricature in a newspaper depicted Tolstoy in a room full of valuables, labeled "property of my wife." He was guzzling rich food and drinking fine wine while starving onlookers held out their skinny hands in vain. This, of course, was far from the truth.

Tolstoy tried to live out his faith in every way he could. It was out of consideration for his wife that he remained home. And this had become no small feat. The flagrant disharmony between his life, beliefs, and conscience, not to mention the increasing madness of his own wife's behavior, had pushed him to the limits on more than one occasion. In a letter to his wife, dated 1897, where he formally announced his intention to leave, he made it clear to her that he was not displeased with her. He simply acknowledged the fact that she was unable — literally unable — to see things and to think as he did. His departure, however, did not take place. He waited another thirteen years.

By the time he finally left home, Sonya had become utterly hysterical — particularly on the subject of publication rights. Justifiably, Sonya worried about securing a financial future, both for herself and for her children. However, her obsession drove her to the brink. She constantly spied upon her husband,

and pretended, from time to time, to have poisoned herself. Her "nerves" eventually led her to a mental breakdown, where she lost all control over herself. When Tolstoy finally left, he genuinely thought he was doing the best thing he could do for his wife. Besides, his dream had always been to spend his last days in material poverty, surrounded by the peasants and workers he loved.

Finally, one night, while lying in bed, the eighty-two-year-old Tolstoy reached a decision. In the predawn hours of October 28, 1910, he secretly left, and with his doctor drove to the train station, leaving Sasha, his youngest daughter, behind to give the news to Sonya. After reading his letter of departure, Sonya ran out of the house, rushed down to the pond, and threw herself into it, whereupon her family immediately hauled her out. Shortly thereafter, Sasha joined her father, who by now was in the Caucasus, at Astopovo, ill and lying in bed with a temperature of 104° at the dingy station-master's house near the railroad.

In the days that followed, the Tolstoy children, one by one, managed to slip in and speak to their dying father. Sonya too managed to come to Tolstoy. Holding her husband's hand and weeping, she whispered, "Forgive me, forgive me." Now near his last breath, Tolstoy could only utter a few deep sighs in response. All the while, news of Tolstoy's impending death had spread. Outside the little cottage the crowds grew. And on November 7, a little over a week after his departure, Tolstoy's life ebbed away.

Truth on Trial

On the day before his death, Tolstoy called out to his son: "Sergei! Sergei! I love Truth... very much... I love Truth." Those were his last words. And in many respects, this was Tolstoy's greatest legacy. Tolstoy was never a saint, nor completely consistent. But he was honest — both with himself and with those around him.

For Tolstoy, Truth was moral. It demanded a radical revolution, a transformation founded on conscience, exercised through a voluntary renunciation of every kind of excess for the sake of justice and peace. Tolstoy dreamt of a revolution from within, one that was unshakeable and ready for any suffering. It is important to remember this, especially in light of his critique of orthodox Christianity. Tolstoy dismissed all the traditional Christian doctrines — the Incarnation, the Resurrection, the Ascension, the miracles of the Gospels and of the saints. But his rejection was not so much on the basis of rationalism, but out of moral outrage. Tolstoy called the suppression of Truth "the Wall of Silence," referring particularly to the teachings of Jesus that had been so effectively silenced that Christians persecute their fellow humans in the name of Christianity. It infuriated him that those who profess Jesus as being divine and infallible were also the very ones who neglected to do the things he actually taught. It is this inconsistency that Tolstoy highlights. Although he replaces this inconsistency with one of his own, replacing a Jesus who is not divine but whose words are, nevertheless, he rightly asked the question Jesus surely would have asked if he had been living during tsarist Russia: How is it that self-professed Christians refuse to obey Christ?

Tolstoy argued that if the moral teaching of Jesus was true, then it made demands upon us, and we would have to change the way we live. The vast abyss existing between the rich, leisured class and that of the pauper classes, along with the existence of wars that ensue over property and resources, was, according to him, unconditionally antithetical to the kingdom Jesus came to bring. In this kingdom, as Tolstoy sees it, there are no nations — only persons who embark on a new way of life and of communion, born of the heart. Only persons who love, who make what is theirs the property of all, can undermine the systems of a war-torn world.

Like Kierkegaard with his three spheres of existence, Tolstoy believed that a person was guided by one of three fundamental religious attitudes. There is first the religion of all the babies, the aesthetic sphere, who want as much milk and warmth as they can get and care about nothing else — the religion of personal, material, social comfort. Then there is the religion of those who see the aim of life in the welfare of the family, clan, tribe, nation, or even of the whole of humanity. We may call this the religion of idealism, or the ethical sphere. Lastly there is the one who recognizes some supreme Law or Lord to be obeyed. Such a person will say: "Let justice be done though the heavens fall" — it is the religion of service of the highest, the genuinely religious sphere.

It is this sphere that solves the riddle of life, for it alone recognizes that life lived for self can never produce happiness. Love, that activity that has for its object the good of others, is the only legitimate manifestation of life. And this "good" is not an ideal, but something that is embedded in the warp and woof of personal existence through personal investment and sacrifice. In his own meager, fallible way, Tolstoy strove to live this out. If leisured and successful folk were put off by his eccentricities, the peasants grew to love him. And there was a reason for this. For many years he plowed a piece of land that belonged to an old widow who had no one to do this job for her. He would also gather the harvest in for her. Whenever Tolstoy was discouraged or sad he would go out to the road that led through the village and help the pilgrims carry their bundles. Far from romanticizing peasant life, Tolstoy genuinely loved those of simple heart.

Tolstoy's attempt to love his neighbor was, of course, not always pure or helpful. "Love," as he came to teach, rarely emerged from his life unscathed, tainted as it was by all his unique character flaws. While in Switzerland, for example, he spent the evening in a hotel at Lucerne. While there he became terribly excited, fuming with indignation, after a musician had played for a long time beneath the balcony where many people were sitting. Everyone enjoyed his playing, but not one offered him a cent when he tried to take a collection. So Tolstoy took the musician by the arm and, seating him at his own table, ordered supper and champagne for him, carrying on as if the musician was a long lost friend. This was typical of Tolstoy — showing both his good and his bad side. In this case, he did the right thing but in the wrong way, being grossly ostentatious in his charity. It was needless for him to show off, let alone embarrass the other patrons in the process.

Tolstoy admittedly was a man plagued by all the sins and foibles that haunt the rest of us. This was no more acutely felt, as we have seen, than in his own home. Tolstoy often exacerbated the conflict with his wife on account of his principled intolerance. He not only allowed his odious, humorless disciples to infest his house and to whisper poison about Sonya in his ears; he also, like her, gave into outbursts of rage.

Of course, it is a rare individual whose life completely coheres with his "profession." And whatever one concludes about Tolstoy's domestic affairs, he did strive to fight against the self-indulgent life and against the privileges belonging to his social class. It would be wrong, therefore, to dismiss Tolstoy's message on account of his personal failings. To live according to conscience is often not pretty, and more often than not misunderstood. This was certainly the case for Tolstoy.

As to what he had to say, readers are invited to read the text that follows and judge Tolstoy's words for themselves. His message evokes a wide range of feeling and opinion, and it is easy to take issue with him on this or that point. However, what is more important to grasp is Tolstoy's overarching stance. Many have accused him of being mired in legalism, committed to an entirely negative ethic, formulated in terms of absolute commands. Others, like G. K. Chesterton, note that because Tolstoy was not a mystic, he had a tendency to go "mad" — like rejecting outright any legitimate role of government.

Still others argue that by jettisoning the miraculous element out of faith, including the redemptive role and significance of Christ and his cross, Tolstoy underestimates the human capacity for sin; he fails to grasp how incapable our human strength is of living by his ideals. Eberhard Arnold is probably correct when he argues that Tolstoy did not possess full insight into the innermost heart and core of Jesus' life:

> Certainly Jesus did say those things that Tolstoy listed as demands; but Jesus compiled no new set of laws. Instead, he witnessed to these things as the life energy that leads to the heart of God. Jesus overcame death through the power of life. In doing this he passed judgment on our life of self. Jesus gave his life for the redemption of our guilt, for the healing of our sick souls. Tolstoy did not find this healing.[7]

In other words, Tolstoy easily points out how we as human beings, along with our institutions, fall short of the ideals of Christ, yet by insisting on an earthly Christ — Christ purged of miracle and terror, of grace and divine abandonment — he has little to say to the despairing, to the slain of the trenches, to the victims of systemic injustice, or to the countless millions who have died as a result of some dictator's death camp.

Tolstoy's prophetic religion was undoubtedly an antidote to the Christian hypocrisy of his day. His counterpart, Dostoyevsky, took a different route, recapturing the holy Redeemer, the Christ who against all logic redeems the sins of the world. Tolstoy, with no less forcefulness, restored Christ's starkest and most revolutionary moral demands. And yet we know from his diary how much Tolstoy revered Dostoyevsky. And one cannot but feel Dostoyevsky's spirit in many of his shorter works, such as *The Death of Ivan Ilych* or *Resurrection*. True, Tolstoy was no mystic, but it is a misjudgment to accuse him of dour moralism. It was not that he wanted to reduce Christ to human terms, but to exalt his true significance for humanity. Eternal life is ultimately felt in working for the happiness of others. Anything less betrays a false faith.

In his short story *Master and Man*, Vasili Andreevich, Nikita's cold-hearted master, saves himself precisely at the point when he decides to lay down his life for Nikita. He finds Nikita already half frozen, dying in their snow-covered sledge, lost in the wilderness on a bitter winter night. Suddenly, pushing Nikita down, he laid down on top of him, covering him not only with his fur coat but with the whole of his body, which glowed with warmth. As he lay there, he no longer could hear the whistling of the wind, but only Nikta's breathing. "There, and you say you are dying! Lie still and get warm, that's our way...." began Vasili, in tears. With a peculiar joy such as he had never felt before, he then began to fall unconscious. And it seemed to him that he was Nikita and Nikita was he, and that his life was not in himself but in Nikita. Tolstoy writes: "He strained his ears and heard Nikita breathing and even slightly snoring. 'Nikita is alive, so I too am alive!' he said to himself triumphantly." And Nikita was kept warm beneath his dead master.

In the end, Tolstoy's diatribes, whether against government, violence, property, or what have you, stem from his great understanding of love — a reality that encompasses a fraternal order rooted in heartfelt sacrifice. The essays and thoughts that follow, taken from his religious and personal writings, must therefore be read against this backdrop, or else one risks taking Tolstoy's words out of context. It is love that ultimately matters. And this love, for Tolstoy, is less a feeling and more a strength — a willingness to give oneself for the well-being of others. Love and Truth are conjoined together, and necessarily so, as both make up the essential faculty of the human soul. But this faculty, if vivisected from God's love, is like a plant without roots. In the end, as Tolstoy writes,

> we can only unite with each other in God. We do not need to take steps toward each other; we need only to approach

God. If there were a huge church in which the light from above fell only in the center, people would only have to go toward the light in the center to be gathered together. Be assured, if we all approach God, we will be drawn toward each other.

Notes

1. Edward Crankshaw, *Tolstoy: The Making of a Novelist* (New York: Viking Press, 1974), 104.

2. A. N. Wilson, *Tolstoy* (New York: Norton, 1988), 204.

3. John Stewart Collins, *Leo Tolstoy* (London: House of Stratus, 2001), 86.

4. Wilson, *Tolstoy,* 361.

5. Ernest Howard Crosby, *Tolstoy and His Message* (New York: Funk & Wagnall, 1904), 29–30.

6. Tatyana Tolstoy, *Tolstoy Remembered* (New York: McGraw-Hill, 1977), 286.

7. Eberhard Arnold, "The Healing of the Life of the Soul" (Farmington, Pa.: Plough Publishing Archives, 1920).

1

The Quest for Meaning

ASHAMED TO LIVE

I would like to say that I'm happy and cheerful, but I can't. I'm not unhappy, far from it, and I've not become feeble yet — still further from it. But I feel miserable. I can't help but notice the life around me, and this life is repulsive.

I went for a walk last night. On the way back I saw a tussle going on and heard a policeman shouting: "Take them away!" I asked what was going on. They had picked up some prostitutes: three were taken away but one was drunk and so dropped behind. I waited. A yardman with a lantern caught up with her: she was a girl of the same build as my thirteen-year-old Masha, in a filthy torn dress, with a hoarse, drunken voice; she wouldn't move and lit a cigarette. "I'll give it to you, you bitch's whelp," the policeman shouted. I looked at her snub-nosed, gray, old, coarse face. I asked how old she was: she was sixteen. Then they took her away.

They took her away. What did I do? Nothing. I didn't take her home, didn't give her a meal, didn't do anything at all for her — but I did grow fond of her. They took her away to the police station to sit in jail till morning, and then to the doctor's to be examined. I went off to my clean and comfortable bed to sleep and read a book (and eat and drink figs and water). What did it all mean?

In the morning I decided to go and see her. I went to the police station, but they had already taken her away. A police officer answered my questions incredulously and explained what they did with people like that. It's a normal thing for them. When I said I was surprised at her youth he said, "There are many younger."

This same morning a lieutenant came around. He had fallen on hard times and now spends the nights in a doss house. He came to me in great agitation. "A terrible thing has happened in our place. A laundry woman lived in our house. She's twenty-two. She couldn't work and had no money to pay for a night's lodgings. The landlady kicked her out. She was ill and hadn't had a square meal for a long time. She wouldn't go away, so a policeman was summoned. He took her away. 'Where can I go,' she said. He said: 'You can die where you like, but you can't live here without any money.' And he sat her down in a church porch. In the evening she had nowhere to go and so she went back to the landlady, but before she could reach the apartment she fell down at the gates and died."

I walked there from the police station. There was a coffin in the cellar, and in the coffin was a barely clothed woman with a stiff leg bent at the knee. Wax candles were burning. A deacon was reading a sort of requiem. I was there out of curiosity.

I'm ashamed to write this, ashamed to live. But this is why I am so miserable. For at home a dish of sturgeon, the fifth course, was found not to be fresh. It was taken away. And my talk about all this terrible need with my friends was greeted with bewilderment — why talk about it if you can't put it right?

So I pray: "God, teach me how to exist, how to live, so that my life should not be so loathsome to me." I'm waiting for Him to teach me.   — *Tolstoy's Letters*

IS THIS LIFE?

From the time we get up in the morning until we go to bed our lives consist of a series of acts. Every day we must decide, from all the possibilities, what it is we will do. But without guidance in the choice of our actions we are lost.

How are we to decide? What will guide us? For the most part we turn to an interminable number of facts and actions that make up what is called propriety, custom, and duty, even sacred duty. We look around us to see what others are doing and believe that the people who do these things know why they are doing them. We become convinced that what we are doing has meaning, if not wholly known to us, at least known to others.

But these very same people whom we look to find themselves in the same situation. They do what they do only because others, who, as it seems to them, have an explanation of these deeds, demand the same from them. And thus, involuntarily deceiving each other, we each become ever more accustomed, not only to these things without understanding why, but become accustomed to ascribing to our deeds some mysterious, incomprehensible meaning. And the less we understand the meaning of what we do, the more dubious these acts become, the more importance we attach to them, and with all the greater solemnity do we carry them out.

Rich and the poor, we all behave and act like those around us and think we are doing our duty, reassuring ourselves by the thought that what has been done for so long by so many people, and is so highly prized by them, cannot but be the real business of life. And we live on to old age, and die, believing that even if we ourselves do not know why we live, why we are here, others know the reason for living — the very people who know precisely as little about it as we who depend upon them.

Add to this, new people come into existence, are born, grow up, and, looking upon this whirlpool of existence called life —

in which old, gray, respected men, surrounded by the reverence of the people, assert that this senseless commotion is life, and that there is no other — go away clueless after being jostled at life's doors. Such a one who has never beheld an assembly of people, having seen a crowding, lively, noisy throng at the entrance, and having decided that this is the assembly itself, after having been elbowed at the door, goes home with aching ribs and under the full conviction that he has actually been in the assembly.

The whole of our complicated, seething activity, with our busyness, our wars, our means of communication, our science and our art, is, for the most part, only the thronging of the clueless crowd about the doorway of life.

We pierce mountains, we fly around the world, we have electricity, microscopes, telephones, wars, parliaments, philanthropy, universities, scholarly societies, museums — but what is it all for? Is this life?   — *On Life*

A CONFESSION

When I got married my search for the meaning of life was completely diverted. My whole life became centered around my family and how to increase our means of livelihood. I tasted the temptation of authorship, as well as the immense monetary rewards and recognition that came with it, and managed to stifle all questions as to the meaning of my own life or life in general.

So I lived, but then something strange began to happen to me. I began to experience moments of perplexity where life "froze," as though I did not know what to do or how to live, and I felt lost and became dejected. But this passed, and I went on living as before. Then these moments of perplexity began to reoccur more and more frequently, and invariably took the same form. When they came, the same questions kept coming to my mind: "Why? What is it for? What does it lead to?"

At first it seemed to me that these were aimless, irrelevant questions. Besides, finding the answers wouldn't be difficult. But these questions kept pressing themselves on me, pounding on me to find an answer. Their persistence was like drops of ink always falling on one place till they ran together into one black blot.

Then something happened to me, which was very much like what occurs to everyone stricken with a mortal disease. At first trivial symptoms of indisposition appear, to which the sick person pays no attention; then these symptoms reappear more and more frequently until they merge into uninterrupted periods of suffering. The suffering increases and, before the sick person can look around, what he took for a mere indisposition has become more important to him than anything else on earth — it is death!

This is exactly what happened to me. I became aware that my condition was not a chance indisposition, but something very serious, and that if all these questions continued to press on me I would have to find an answer to them. But the questions seemed so foolish, so simple, so childish, and yet, no sooner had I taken hold of them and attempted to answer them than I was convinced, first, that they were neither childish nor silly, but were concerned with the deepest problems of life, and, in the second place, try as I would, I was unable to solve them.

I was determined, however, to figure out *why* I was living as I was. As long as I did not know the reason *why* I could not do anything, I could not live. While thinking about the management of my household and estate, which greatly preoccupied me at that time, the question would suddenly occur: "Well, you have five thousands acres of land, and three hundred horses — What then? So what?"

I was absolutely muddled up inside, and did not know what to think. When thinking about how best to educate my children,

I would ask myself: "What for?" Or when thinking about how best to promote the welfare of the peasants, I would suddenly say to myself: "But what does it matter to me?" And when I thought about the fame that all my literary works would bring to me, I would say to myself: "Very well, I will become famous. So what? What then?"

I could find no answers, but the questions would not wait. They had to be answered at once, and if I did not answer them, it was impossible for me live. But no answer was being given. I felt that the ground on which I stood was crumbling, that there was nothing for me to stand on, that what I had been living from and for was nothing, that I had no solid reason for living.

My life then came to a standstill. I could breathe, eat, drink, and sleep, for I could not help doing these things. But there was no real life in me because I did not have a single desire, the fulfillment of which I could feel to be reasonable. If I wished for anything, I knew beforehand that, were I to satisfy the wish, or were I not to satisfy it, nothing would come of it. Had a fairy appeared and offered me anything I desired, I wouldn't have known what to say.

I couldn't even wish to know the truth, because I surmised that life was ultimately meaningless. Every day of life, every step in it, brought me, as it were, nearer the precipice, and I saw clearly that before me there was nothing but ruin. And to stop was impossible; to go back was impossible; and it was impossible to shut my eyes so as not to see that there was nothing before me but suffering and death, absolute annihilation.

•

So here I was, a healthy, fortunate man, but with no reason for living. As a result, an irresistible power compelled me to rid myself one way or other of life. I cannot say I *wished* to kill myself. The power that drew me away from life was stronger, fuller, and more widespread than any mere wish. It was a force similar to that of wanting to live, only in a contrary direction.

All my strength drew me away from life. The thought of self-destruction now came to me as naturally as thoughts of how to improve my life had come formerly. And it was so seductive that I had to be cunning with myself lest I should carry it out too hastily.

Besides, I still wanted to do everything possible to disentangle the matter. "If I cannot unravel these riddles now, there will always be time." And it was then that I, a man blessed by fortune, hid a cord from myself lest I should hang myself from the crosspiece of the partition in my room where I undressed alone every evening. I also ceased to go out shooting with a gun lest I should be tempted by so easy a way of ending my life. I did not know what I wanted: I feared life, desired to escape from it, yet still hoped for something.

There is a tale, told long ago, of a traveler overtaken on a plain by an enraged beast. In trying to escape from the beast he crawls into a dry well, but immediately sees that at the bottom of the well is a dragon with open jaws ready to swallow him. And the unfortunate man, not daring to climb out lest he should be destroyed by the enraged beast, and not daring to leap to the bottom of the well lest he should be eaten by the dragon, seizes a twig growing in a crack in the well and clings to it. His hands are growing weaker and he feels he will soon have to resign himself to the destruction that awaits him above or below; but still he clings on.

Then he sees two mice, a black one and a white one, going regularly around and around the stem of the twig to which he is clinging and gnawing at it. And soon the twig will snap and he will fall into the dragon's jaws. The traveler knows that he will inevitably perish; but while still hanging on he looks around, sees some drops of honey on the leaves of the twig, reaches them with his tongue and licks them.

So I too clung to the twig of life, knowing that the dragon of death was awaiting me, ready to tear me to pieces; and I could not understand why I had fallen into such torment.

I tried to lick the honey that formerly consoled me, but the honey no longer gave me pleasure, and the white and black mice of day and night gnawed at the branch by which I hung. I saw the dragon clearly and the honey no longer tasted sweet. I only saw the inescapable dragon and the mice, and I could not tear my gaze from them. And this is not a fable but the real unanswerable predicament that faces every human being.

The deception of the joys of life that formerly relieved my terror of the dragon now no longer deceived me. The two drops of honey that diverted my eyes from the cruel truth of my existence, my love of family and of writing, were no longer sweet to me.

"Family"...I said to myself. But my wife and children are also human. They are placed just as I am: they must either live in a lie or see the terrible truth. Why should they live? Why should I love them, protect them, nurture them? Loving them, I cannot hide the truth from them: each step in knowledge leads them to the truth. And the truth is death.

But what about "writing"? Wasn't this one thing I could do that could escape the clutches of death? But soon I saw that this too was a fraud. As long as I believed that life had meaning, though one I could not express, the reflection of life in writing afforded me pleasure. It was pleasant to look at life in the mirror of literary works. But once I began to seek the meaning of my life, I could no longer soothe myself with what I now saw in the mirror, namely, that my life made no sense and was desperate. Once I grasped how meaningless and terrible my own life was, the play in the mirror could no longer amuse me. No sweetness of honey could be sweet to me once I saw the dragon and saw the mice gnawing away my support.

But this was not all. Had I simply understood that life had no meaning I could have borne it quietly, knowing that this was my lot. But I could not satisfy myself with that. Had I been like a man living in a jungle in which there was no exit, I could have lived. But I was like one lost in a jungle who, horrified at having lost his way, rushes about wishing to find the path. He knows that each step he takes confuses him even more, but still he cannot help rushing about. In my search for answers to life's questions I experienced just what a person feels when lost in a forest. He reaches a glade, climbs a tree, and clearly sees the limitless distance, but sees that his home is not and cannot be there. Then he goes into the dark wood and sees only the darkness; his home is not there.

My life was indeed terrible. And to rid myself of the terror I was ready to kill myself. I felt a horror of what awaited me and knew that it was more horrible than the position I was in. Yet I could not just wait patiently for the end. The horror of the darkness was too great to bear, and I longed to free myself from it as quickly as possible with a rope or a bullet. This was the feeling that, above all, drew me to the brink of suicide.

•

My question — that which at the age of fifty brought me to the verge of suicide — was the simplest of questions, a question lying in the soul of every person. It was a question without an answer to which one cannot live, as I had found by experience. It was: "What will come of what I am doing today or shall do tomorrow? What will come of my life? What is life for?"

Differently expressed, the question is: "Why should I live, why hope for anything, or do anything?" It can also be expressed thus: "Does my life have any meaning that death cannot destroy?"

To this one question, variously expressed, I sought an answer in philosophy and science. According to philosophy, the essence of life and all that exists, is designated as "idea," or "substance," or "spirit," or "will." It's all one and the same: that the essence of life exists and that I am of that same essence.

But why this essence exists the philosopher does not know, and does not say, if he is a careful enough thinker. I ask: "Why should this essence exist? What results from the fact that it is and will be?" Philosophy not only cannot answer this question, but can only put forth the same question. If it keeps firmly to its proper sphere, it can only answer the question, "What am I, and what is the universe?" by saying, "All and nothing," and to the question, "Why?" by adding, "I do not know."

When I turned to the study of science the result was the same. "What is the meaning of my life?" "There is none." Or: "What will come of my life?" "Nothing." Or: "Why does everything exist that exists, and why do I exist?" "Because it exists."

I fared no better in turning to the more exact sciences. "What is the meaning of my life?" The biologist answers: "You are what you call your 'life'; you are a transitory, causal cohesion of particles. The mutual interactions and changes of these particles produce in you what you call your 'life'. That cohesion will last some time; afterward the interaction of these particles will cease and what you call 'life' will cease, and so will all your questions. You are an accidentally united little lump of energy. That little lump undergoes decomposition, which we call 'life'; the lump disintegrates, decomposition ends, and with it all the questions."

So answers the scientist.

What I found in philosophy and science I confronted elsewhere among history's sages. For Socrates, life in the body was a deception. Its destruction was thus a blessing, and we should desire it. According to Solomon, everything in the world — folly and wisdom and riches and poverty and mirth and grief — all was vanity and empty. We die and nothing is left of us. It is all very senseless. For the Buddha, we must ultimately free ourselves from life, as life itself consists of suffering. For Schopenhauer, life is something that should not exist at all; it is an evil. Only the passage into Nothingness is good. And what these thinkers have said has been said and thought and felt by millions upon millions of people like them. I too have thought it and felt it.

So my search in philosophy and among the sciences and sages of history, far from freeing me from my despair, only increased it. All was vanity! Happy is he who has not been born. Death is better than life, and one must free oneself from this life.

•

I then turned my attention to the people around me, hoping to find an answer from them. I began to observe how people like myself lived, and what their attitude was to this question that brought me into such despair.

Some simply asserted that life was an absurdity. There was no answer to life's questions. Others, the majority, argued that while life had no ultimate meaning, one should just eat, drink, and be merry. Still others argued that life consisted in strength and power, in destroying life. The absurdity of life could be overcome by taking one's own life in defiance, promptly ending the stupid joke. Though small in number, more and more in our circle were choosing this path. Finally, some admitted that life had no meaning, but in weakness we had to pretend that it did. In short, among my peers the terrible contradiction of life was simply evaded.

I could no longer do this. Had I enough courage I would have ended my life, but I see now that I didn't kill myself because inside me there was a dim awareness that something was not quite right in the way I was approaching my dilemma. I knew that my very act of thinking affirmed the validity of my life. Or to put it another way: were there no life, reason itself would not exist. Reason was life's son. Reason was the fruit of life, yet my reason rejected life itself. Something was wrong here.

There was another thing that nagged me. It was easy to see the pointlessness of living, yet the simplest, most down-to-earth folk around me lived and did so believing that life had meaning. How was this? How did they possess a sense of meaning when all I could conclude was life was pointless?

I instinctively felt that if I wished to live and understand the meaning of life, I must seek this meaning not among my cultured peers, those who lived for no satisfactory reason, but among the masses of those simple, uneducated, and poor people who live and affirm life's meaning, despite the conclusions delivered by reason. Their lives, though rationally groundless, had purpose. They lived by a faith that I, in all my reasonableness, had rejected.

With this realization, however, my situation became even worse. The path of reason led me to reject life. Yet to turn to faith demanded that I deny reason, which was yet more impossible for me than a denial of life. To understand the meaning of life I would have to turn to faith, but to do this I would also have to renounce my reason — the very thing for which alone meaning could be determined. And yet I had to admit that besides rational knowledge there seemed to exist a kind of knowledge — faith — that enabled people to live and that provided them answers to the questions I was asking.

And then it dawned on me that in order to live at all one must believe in something. Faith was the strength of life. Without believing that life was worth living, we would not live. And if I did not acknowledge the illusory nature of the finite, then I had to believe in the finite; or, if I saw the illusory nature of the finite, then I had to believe in the Infinite. Either way, I realized that no one lives without faith, not even the strictest rationalist.

•

My new realization about the necessity of faith forced me to go back to my original question, which, in turn, helped me to see that the answer I wanted had to do with the Infinite's relation to the finite, and vice versa. What I needed to know was what the meaning of my life had *beyond* time and space, and not what my life meant within the confines of time and space. The answer to that, of course, was: "None."

By appealing only to reason I could not get myself out of the quagmire of finitude, and thus life was meaningless. But by faith I could find an answer to life's meaning. For faith alone offered the key to understanding why life was worth living and why it was we instinctively don't end our own lives. Faith pointed me away from myself to the Infinite, of which I was a part.

What I eventually discovered was that the conception of an infinite God, along with the divinity of the soul, the connection of human affairs with God, the unity and existence of the soul, and our conception of moral goodness and evil — that all of these are hidden in the infinity of human thought. They are the very things without which neither life nor I would exist.

With Solomon, I began to understood that *our* wisdom was folly. I also saw that reason by itself always ran in a vicious circle, like a cogwheel the teeth of which no longer catch in another. However much and however well we may be able to reason we cannot get an answer to our question by reason alone; it will always be $0 = 0$. Finally, I began to grasp that the answers given by faith were stored up in the deepest recesses of human wisdom and that I had no right to deny them on the basis of reason, and that those answers were the only ones that truly solved life's riddle.

So the key to my quest was faith. But not the faith of my self-indulgent peers. These "believers," like myself, lived in comfort and ease while still being gripped by a fear of suffering and death. Like myself, they lived to satisfy their desires and lived just as badly, if not worse, than those who didn't profess any faith. No arguments could convince me of the truth of their faith. Only deeds that would free me from what I dreaded — poverty, sickness, and death — could convince me. And so I turned to the faith of the common people and to those outside the church.

The more I looked at their life the more I became convinced that they were the ones, despite their various superstitions, who had real faith. I found, contrary to those in my own circle, that these folks were content with life — despite a life of heavy labor and hardship. In complete contrast to their ignorance, they knew the meaning of life and death, labored quietly, endured deprivations and suffering, and lived and died seeing therein not vanity but good. And after living among these folks for several years I understood that *that* is life itself, and that the meaning given to that life was truth: and I accepted it.

•

How then was I able to return to my original faith, the one I once held when I was younger but later rejected? What repelled me in the past, as I discovered, was not the faith but the meaninglessness of those lives who lived in contradiction to the faith they professed. This included my own. I went astray not because I erred in my thinking but because I lived badly. It was not an error in my thought that hid the truth from me so much as my life itself, with its epicurean pursuit of satisfying one's pleasures. I asked myself what my life amounted to and got the reply: an evil and an absurdity. And so it was.

But then I made the mistake of concluding that life in general was absurd. I loved the darkness more than the light, but instead of recognizing this I lashed out at life itself. The truth was always as true as that two and two are four, but I refused to acknowledge it, because on admitting two and two to be four I had also to admit that my life was bad and that it was I who had made it so. But I could not do this. I felt I was a good person.

But then I came to love good, honest people. Now everything became clear to me. Compared to them, I had been living as a parasite. My comfort, my welfare, and all my learned discussions were at the expense of those who really earned their living. Yet it was these very people who knew how to live and were happy, not I.

If a naked, hungry beggar has been taken from the crossroads, brought into a building belonging to a beautiful establishment, fed, supplied with drink, and made to move a handle up and down, it is evident that the beggar, before seeking to know why he was taken, why he should work the handle, and whether the arrangements of the establishment are reasonable or not, must first move the handle. If he moves the handle he will understand that it works a pump, that the pump draws water, and that the water irrigates the garden beds. Then he will be taken from the pumping station to another place where he will gather fruits and will enter into the joy of his master, and, passing from lower to higher work, will understand better and better the arrangements of the whole establishment; and he will take part with them without once stopping to ask why he is there, nor will he ever think of reproaching the master of that place.

So it is with those who do the will of their master, the simple, uneducated working folk, whom so many of us educated ones regard as cattle. They do not reproach the master, but we, the wise, eat the master's food but do not do what the master wishes, and instead of doing it sit in a circle and discuss: "Why should that handle be moved? Isn't it stupid to move such a handle?" And when we have thought it all out, what is our conclusion? Why, that the master is stupid or that he doesn't even exist, while we wise ones ultimately feel we are fit for nothing, and that we must somehow or other end our lives.

The conviction that the truth could only be found by living it eventually led me to doubt the rightness of my own life. I began to understand that to grasp life's meaning I had to stop living like a parasite and live a real life. I also had to heed more attentively to my heart, from which my search for God needed to proceed. For I knew that any conception of God I might have would still be but a conception, one that I could evoke or refrain from evoking in myself. That was not what I wanted to seek. I wanted that without which there could be no life. Only then could I truly live. For based on fading memories of my past, I only lived, really lived, when I felt him and sought him with my whole heart.

And then finally, more than ever before, everything within me and around me lit up. "What more did I have to seek?" exclaimed a voice within me. "This is He. God is that without which you cannot live. To know God and to live is one and the same thing! God is life. Live seeking God, and then you will not live without God." This light that had dawned inside and around me never again abandoned me. And I was saved.

•

I had come full circle. In short, what happened to me was something like this: I was put into a boat and pushed off from an unknown shore, shown the direction to the opposite shore, had oars put into my unskilled hands, and was left alone. I rowed as best I could and moved forward, but the further I advanced toward the middle of the stream, the more rapidly grew the current, bearing me away from my goal. More and more I encounter others, like myself, borne away by the stream.

There were a few rowers who continued to row, but then there were others who had abandoned their oars. There were large boats and immense vessels full of people. Some struggled against the current, others yielded to it. And the further I went, the more, as I watched the long line floating down the current, I forgot the course pointed out to me as my own.

In the very middle of the stream, amid the crowd of boats and vessels floating down, I had altogether lost the course and so threw down my oars. From all sides the joyful and exulting navigators, as they rowed or sailed downstream, assured me — and each other — that no other direction was possible. And I believed them and floated right along. And I was carried far, so far that I heard the roar of the rapids in which I was bound to perish, and I could even see boats that had been shattered from them.

Then I came to my senses. It was long before I clearly comprehended what had happened to me. I saw before me nothing but destruction, toward which I was rushing, which I dreaded. I saw no safety anywhere and did not know what to do!

Yet on looking back, I saw a countless number of boats engaged in a ceaseless struggle against the force of the torrent. Then I remembered the shore, the oars, and the course, and at once I began to row hard up the stream and again toward the shore. That shore was God, that course was the wisdom of the Ages, those oars were the free will given me to make for the shore and unite with God. And so the force of life was renewed in me and I again began to live.   — *My Confession*

I, LIKE THE THIEF

Five years ago I came to believe in Christ's teachings, and my life suddenly changed. I ceased to desire what I had previously desired and began to desire what I formerly did not want. What had previously seemed to me good seemed evil, and what seemed evil seemed good. It happened to me as it happens to a man who goes out on some business and suddenly decides that the business is unnecessary and returns home. All that was on his left is now on his right; his former wish to get as far as possible from home has changed into a wish to be as near as possible to it. The direction of my life and my desires became different, and good and evil changed places.

I, like that thief on the cross, have believed Christ's teaching and been saved. This is no far-fetched comparison, but the closest expression of the condition of spiritual despair and horror at the problem of life and death in which I lived formerly, and of the condition of peace and happiness in which I am now. I, like the thief, knew that I had lived and was living badly. I, like the thief, knew that I was unhappy and suffering. I, like the thief to the cross, was nailed by some force to a life of suffering and evil. And as, after the meaningless sufferings and evils of life, the thief awaited the terrible darkness of death, so did I await the same thing.

In all this I was exactly like the thief, but the difference was that the thief was already dying, while I was still living. The thief might believe that his salvation lay there beyond the grave, but I could not be satisfied with that, because besides a life beyond the grave, life still awaited me here. And I did not understand that life. It seemed to me terrible. But suddenly I heard the words of Christ and understood them, and life and death ceased to seem evil, and instead of despair I experienced happiness and the joy of life undisturbed by death.

— What I Believe

THE TRUTH THAT SETS FREE

Every person, somewhere during his life, finds himself in regard to truth in the position of one walking in the darkness with light thrown before him by the lantern he carries. He does not see what is not yet lighted up by the lantern. He does not see what he has passed which is hidden in the darkness. Yet at every stage of his journey he sees what is lighted up by the lantern, and he can always choose one side of the road or the other.

All the difficulty and seeming insolubility of the question of freedom results from trying to solve the question by imagining our situation as being stationary in our relation to the truth. We are certainly not free if we imagine ourselves being stationary, and if we forget that our life is but a continual movement from darkness into light, from a lower stage of truth to a higher, from a truth more alloyed with errors to a truth more purified from them.

We would not be free if we knew no truth at all, and in the same way we would not be free and would not even have the notion of freedom if the whole truth, which was to guide us in life, had been revealed once and for all to us in all its purity. But we are not stationary in regard to truth. Each of us is passing through life, and we are continually confronted with learning to know a greater and greater degree of truth, and growing more and more free from error.

Our liberty does not consist in the power of acting independently of the progress of life and the influences arising from it, but in the capacity for recognizing and acknowledging the truth revealed to us, and becoming the joyful participator in the eternal and infinite work of God in the world. Failing this, and refusing to recognize the truth, we become a miserable and reluctant slave dragged where we have no desire to go.

Truth not only points out the way along which we ought to move, but reveals the only way in which to move. And therefore all of us must willingly or unwillingly move along the way of truth, some spontaneously accomplishing the task set us in life, others submitting involuntarily to the law of life. Our freedom lies in the power of this choice. And more than that, this freedom is the sole means of accomplishing the divine work of the life of the world.   — *The Kingdom of God Is within You*

THE MILLER

Imagine a man whose only means of livelihood is a mill. It just so happens that this man begins to hear different ideas about the mill's mechanism, and so he begins to reflect upon the construction of the mill and observe what part is turned by what other part. From the flywheel to the grindstone, from the grindstone to the millrace, from the millrace to the wheel, from the wheel to the gate, the dam, and the water, he comes clearly to conclude that the whole mill operation lies in the dam and the river.

The man rejoices so greatly in his discovery that instead of examining, as he did before, the quality of the flour which comes forth, instead of raising and lowering the millstones, of shoeing them, of tightening and slackening the belt, he begins to study the river. As a result, the mill is thrown entirely out of gear. The people begin to tell the miller that he is not doing his work properly. Yet he argues with them and continues to study the river. He studies the river so much that he finally becomes convinced that the river is the mill itself.

To those who try and prove the faultiness of his course of reasoning, the miller replies, "No mill grinds without water. Consequently, in order to know the mill, it is necessary to know how the water works, to know the force of its current as well as its source. To know the mill, it is necessary to know the river."

The miller cannot be logically dislodged from his line of reasoning. The only means of dispelling his illusion is to show him that good reasoning depends first of all on the object, or on one's objective. This determines the order in which the separate trains of thought are to be arranged, in order that they can be understood. Reasoning not bound together by a common aim is foolish, no matter how logical it may be.

The aim of the miller consists in producing good flour, and this aim, if he will keep it in view, will determine how best to understand the workings of the mill — about the millstones, the wheel, the dam, and also the river. But without this relation to the aim, the miller's arguments, no matter how fine and logical they may be, will be inherently irregular and, what is the principal consideration, useless.

And such, in my opinion, are the arguments addressing the contemporary approach to life.

Life is the mill that we desire to investigate. The mill is necessary to grind well, to produce flour; life is necessary in order that it may be good and for the good. We cannot abandon the quest of understanding for a single moment with impunity. If we abandon it, our deliberations infallibly lose their place.

For this reason, we should study life in order that it might become better, more fruitful. Those who have already sincerely contemplated life's meaning, history's sages, have helped to advance humanity in the path of wisdom. But there have always existed, and there exist now, so-called philosophers and theologians who have abandoned the real aim of reasoning, and who, in its stead, investigate questions unrelated to life — as to why the mill turns. Some assert that it is by reason of the water, others, that it is in consequence of the arrangement. The dispute is heated, and the subject of discussion just moves farther and farther away, and is completely replaced by utterly pointless and obscure topics.

There is an ancient jest about a dispute between a Jew and a Christian. The story runs that the Christian, replying to the confused subtleties of the Jew, slapped the latter on his bald pate with his palm, so that it cracked. He then put forth the following question: "Did the crack come from the pate or from the palm?" At this, their dispute about matters of faith was replaced by a fresh and insoluble problem.

Something of the same sort always happens when it comes to questions about life. The scientific mentality, for instance, is preoccupied with the origin of life. Does it consist of an immaterial beginning, or from the combination of various forms of matter? In science, especially, there is no end to these kinds of questions. All the while, the aim of life's quest gets abandoned.

If our understanding of life is not first implanted within us, then science, or any other branch of knowledge, will be erroneous. It will be as useless as it is aimless. It is not "science" that determines life's meaning, but our conception of life that determines what should be acknowledged as science. And therefore, in order that science may be science, that is, knowledge that helps life along, the question must first be settled as to what is, and what is not science, and to this end our idea of life must be elucidated. This is the greatest task.   — *On Life*

DEATH COMES KNOCKING

Whatever names we dignify ourselves with, whatever uniforms we wear, whatever clergy we have ourselves blessed by, however many millions we possess, however many police are stationed along our streets, however many so-called criminals, revolutionaries, and subversives we punish, whatever exploits we have performed, whatever states we may have founded, buildings we may have erected — from Babel to the Eiffel Tower — there are two inevitable conditions of life, confronting all of us: (1) death, which may at any moment pounce upon any one of us, and (2) the transitoriness of all our works, which so soon pass away and leave no trace.

Whatever we may do — found companies, build palaces and monuments, write songs and poems — none of it remains for long. Soon it passes away, leaving no trace. And therefore, however we may conceal it from ourselves, we cannot help seeing that the significance of our life cannot lie in our personal fleshly existence, the prey of incurable suffering and inevitable death, nor in any social institution or organization. Whoever you are reading these lines, think of your position and of your duties — not of your position as landowner, businessman, lawyer, politician, minister, soldier, which has been temporarily allotted you by society, and not of the imaginary duties laid on you by those positions, but of your real position in eternity as a creature who, at the will of Someone, has been called out of unconsciousness after an eternity of nonexistence to which you may return at any moment at his will.

Think of your real duties, the duties that follow from your real position as a being called into life and endowed with reason and love.

Are you doing what God has sent you into the world for, and to whom you will soon return? Are you doing what he wills? Are you doing his will, when as landowner or entrepreneur you rob the poor of the fruits of their toil, basing your life on this plunder of the workers, or when, as judge or governor, you sentence them to execution, or when as soldiers you prepare for war, killing, and plunder?

Even if you are told that all this is necessary for maintaining the existing order, and that greater disasters would ensue if the way things are were destroyed, isn't it obvious that all this is said by those who profit by such an arrangement, while those who suffer from it — and they are ten times as numerous — think to the contrary? And at the bottom of your heart you know yourself that it is not true, that the existing order of things is not how things are supposed to be.

More importantly, even if such a life is necessary, why do you believe it is *your* duty to maintain it at the cost of your best feelings? Who has made you the nurse in charge of this sick and moribund system? Not society nor the state nor anyone. No one has asked you to undertake this. You who fill your position of landowner, businessman, politician, priest, or soldier know very well that you occupy that position not because you are so concerned about other people's happiness, but simply to satisfy your own interests, to satisfy your own security and well-being. If you did not desire that position, you would not be doing your utmost to retain it.

Try the experiment of ceasing to compromise your conscience in order to retain your position, and you will lose it at once. Think about it.   — *The Kingdom of God Is within You*

WHY IS THIS?

Every one of us wants to love and be loved. Why then, after so many thousand of years, has humankind, though knowing the means of happiness, failed to practice it? Why does the sentiment of love, so natural and so beneficent, fail to rule our lives?

It is obvious that is it not enough to say: Love one another. That has been said for centuries, and has been repeated *ad nauseam,* in all tones, from all platforms, religious and secular. And yet we continue to war instead of love one another. Why is this? No one can doubt that if we — instead of tearing one another to pieces each seeking our own happiness, that of our family, or that of or country — would but help one another, if we would replace selfishness by love and would organize our lives to build up community instead of self-interest, if we loved one another as each of us loves ourselves, if, at least, we did not do to others what we would not like done to us, as was said two thousand years ago, our happiness would be far greater, and human life in general would be reasonable, instead of being what it is now, a succession of contradictions and sufferings.

Most decent human beings acknowledge, if not the law of love, at least the obligation "not to do to others what they would not that others do to them." But even with this we fail to act upon it. Evidently some secret but overwhelming reason prevents us from doing what is ultimately to our advantage, what would save us from the perils that menace us, and what the law of God and our conscience alike dictate. Are we to conclude that love applied to life is a chimera? If so, how is it that for so many centuries we have allowed ourselves to be deluded by this unrealizable ideal? We can neither resolve to follow the law of love in our lives nor to give up the idea.

Why is this? What is the reason for this enduring contradiction? Do we simply lack the desire or is it because we lack the possibility to do what our hearts tell us? Are we just too busy, too engrossed in work, too distracted to pause and collect our thoughts and reflect on what truly ought to be? Why is this?

— Stop and Think

KILLING CONSCIENCE

We are both spiritual and physical in nature. We may thus be moved by things that influence our spiritual nature, or by things that influence our physical nature, as a clock may be moved by its hands or by its main wheel. And just as it is best to regulate the movement of a clock by means of its inner mechanism, so we are best regulated by means of our conscience. Unfortunately, too many of us care less about whether our conscience is working properly than about whether it should appear to be working right. In fact, we deliberately make use of substances in order to keep our conscience working at all.

Why do people drink and get high? Why do we spend ourselves on outer diversions and distractions? It is not to cheer ourselves up, or because it is pleasant to do so, but in order to drown the voice of conscience in ourselves. And this always leads to devastating consequences. Think for a moment what a building would be like if it was erected by people who did not use a straight plumb-rule or right-angled square. The walls would never be perpendicular nor the corners correct. What good would it be to use a soft rule that would bend to suit all the irregularities in the walls, or a square that expanded to fit any angle, acute or obtuse? But this kind of thing happens whenever we dull ourselves and fail to heed our conscience by making use of intoxicants.

Each of us at various periods of life is confronted with certain moral questions that need to be solved. It takes a great deal of effort to attend to them and to seek answers. In every labor, especially at the beginning, there is a time when the work is painfully difficult, when we are tempted to give up. Physical work is painful at first, mental work still more. As Lessing says: people are inclined to cease to think at the point at which thought begins to be difficult; but it is just there, I would add, that thinking begins to be fruitful.

We often feel that it takes too much work to decide the important questions of life. We are thus inclined to evade them. We will do anything to avoid the struggle. By drinking and getting high, or by becoming obsessed with trivial objects and activities, we try, even if unconsciously, to drive from our consciousness these very questions. For these questions torment us, and in order to avoid the disquietude evoked by them, we excite our senses so as to deaden ourselves inside. Eventually, our conscience ceases to demand a solution to the riddles of life, and for months, years, even for a whole lifetime, we can stand before those same moral questions and not be a step closer to their solution. Yet it is in the solution of these moral questions that life's whole movement consists.

We each want to be happy. But we are like the person who needs to see to the bottom of some muddy water to obtain a precious pearl, but who is also afraid of having to dive deep down to get it. So instead of leaping off the edge, we take a stick and stir up the water the moment it begins to settle and become clear. In this way we never quite see where the pearl lies. Isn't this what we each do with our conscience? We muddy the waters of our soul, and, as the years go by, we never break through to life's real meaning. Instead, the sharp point of truth is so blunted that it no longer enables our conscience to do its work.

When we do not live as our conscience demands, and then try to deaden its voice by means of various poisons and fleshly pursuits, we gradually lose the strength to live according to the truth. And to our shame, we become like a person who covers his eyes to hide from himself what he does not wish to see. The diversions we pursue may distract our attention away from conscience, but only for a while. Either we will turn and begin to take heed, or else we will go on disregarding the indications and warnings of our conscience and end up with stale lives of discord and misery.
                                                              — *Essays and Letters*

WHAT MUST BE DONE?

To the question, "What must be done?" I reply first of all that we must cease deceiving others as well as ourselves. We must stop being afraid of the truth, whatever it might be. This comes down to little things: "Not at home," when I am in; "Very well," when I am not that at all; "Not enough time," when we know there is. But there is something more vital here. And this is the matter of how we deceive ourselves. It is this lie that must be overcome if we wish to answer the question, "What must be done?"

How can I truly answer this question if my life is based upon a lie, and when I carefully cast this lie as if it were truth, to others and to myself? Not to lie, in this sense, means not to be afraid of truth; not to invent excuses, and not to accept the excuses of others. It means living according to one's conscience and not being afraid of living in contradiction to all that is false, however dreadful the consequences of doing so might be.

Pretending to others, whether consisting of conventional half-truths or outright lies, is always disadvantageous in the long run. Wisdom alone tells us this much. But lying to one's self leads to complete ruin.

If I consider a wrong road to be a right one, then my every step only leads me farther from my aim. If I have been walking for a long time on a wrong path, I may yet discover that it is the wrong one. But if I, being afraid of the thought of how far I have gone astray, try to assure myself that I may, by following this wrong way a bit further, still come across the right one, then surely I will never find it. If I am afraid of the truth, and then, on seeing it, refuse to acknowledge it, and instead take further steps away from it, I will never come to know what is to be done in life.

If we would only avoid deceiving ourselves, we would find out what to do, where to go, how to live, and do so with clarity. But how can we learn to come to terms with ourselves?

The answer lies in repentance. We must entirely change the esti-mation we have ourselves and how we are living. Instead of viewing our lives as decent and competent, we must acknowl-edge them as being harmful and trifling. Instead of resting on how much we think we know, we should feel how ignorant we are. Instead of imagining ourselves as being kind and good, we must see how hard-hearted we are. And instead of seeing how important we are, we must see our own insignificance.

Without repentance we will think of ourselves as somehow special or exceptional, above others, able to serve them as if we ourselves lacked nothing. Not until we see ourselves as ruined are we able to benefit others. For those of us who have been given much, we especially must lay aside our pride about our education, our cultural sophistication, our talents and skills, and let go of the idea that we are the benefactors of society. No, it is we who have been stealing from humanity. We are the guilty ones for the world's suffering. We are good-for-nothing people. We are not benefactors of the people, but offenders who humiliate them.

The question should be put thus: "How can I, a helpless, use-less person, seeing now the misfortune of having lost my best years, rectify my life and truly serve others?" How can I really turn over a new leaf?

A person will never be able to answer the question, "What must be done?" until he stops deceiving himself and repents. And repentance is not dreadful, even as truth is not dreadful, at least not to those who seek a life that leads to the good.

— *What Is to Be Done?*

STOP, LOOK, CONSIDER!

If I were asked for the most important advice I could give, that which I considered to be the most useful to the people of our time, I would simply say: In the name of God, stop a moment, cease your work, look around you, consider what you are and what you ought to be — think of the ideal!

The ideal is neither something supernatural nor the realm of the unexplained. It appeals to our conscience with more certainty than anything else. The ideal in geometry is the perfectly straight line, and the circle, the radii of which are equal. In science it is exact truths. In morals it is perfect virtue, excellence. Although all these things — straight line, exact truth, perfect virtue — have never existed, they are not only more natural, more known, and more explicable than all our other knowledge, they are also the only things we truly know.

It is said that reality is that which exists. Or, to put it differently, only what exists is real. However, the contrary is the case. True reality, that which we indubitably know, has itself never yet "existed." The ideal is the only thing we know with certainty, but it doesn't actually exist. Yet it is only thanks to the ideal that we know anything at all. The ideal alone can guide us, both individually and collectively.

The Christian ideal — the law of love — has been before us for centuries, and it shines in our time with such intensity that it is virtually impossible to avoid seeing that our problems proceed from that fact that we do not reach for it.

There are those who wish to discount this ideal because it is, as history proves, unattainable. They want to persuade us to close our eyes so as not to see it. They claim that in order to be absolutely certain of arriving safely in port, we ought, before all else, to throw overboard the compass and forge straight ahead. Now we resemble people who, desiring to pull down some object that annoys them, drag at it in opposite directions and have no time to agree as to the direction in which we ought to pull.

Should we then just throw out the ideal? Where would this leave us?

But let us stop all our activity for a moment and consider — comparing the demands of our reason and of our heart with the actual conditions of our lives — in order to see how our whole life and our every action are in incessant and outrageous contradiction to the yearnings of our soul.

Before we can change our way of living and feeling, we must undergo a change in our way of thinking. But before this can happen we must stop and give proper attention to our lives. To hear what those who wish to save us are shouting, we who run singing toward the precipice must cease our hubbub and stop short.

So let us pause and reflect on the state of our lives. If we do, we can't help but be turned toward the ideal. We will grasp anew a conception of life so natural, so simple, so fresh that the needs of our heart and mind will resonate with gladness; we will spontaneously feel what it is that will liberate us from the complications and entanglements of our life and work.

— *On Life*

2

The Law of Love

LIVING WATER

Christ shows us the way to life, and those who embark on this way are like a fountain of living water bubbling forth from the earth, which steadily moves in all directions in spite of the obstacles blocking it. One who follows Christ's way can just as little ask what he must positively do as the spring of water flowing from the earth can ask such a question. It flows, refreshing the soil, the earth, the trees, the birds, the animals, and people. The same is true for the one who genuinely believes in Christ.

If we believe in Christ we will not ask him what he wants us to do. The love that constitutes the force of our life will faithfully and undoubtedly show us where we must act and what we must do. Christ clearly points the way: to love, to feed the hungry, give drink to the thirsty, cloth the naked, visit those imprisoned. Conscience alone compels us to deliver our fellow humans from suffering and its causes.

Just as a spring cannot ask where it is to send its water, whether it shall spurt up on the grass and the leaves of the trees, or trickle down to the roots of the grass and the trees, so those who believe in the truth cannot ask what they must do first of all — whether to teach the poor, defend them, bring them joy, supply them with life's pleasures, or support them when they are perishing from need.

And just as the spring of water flows down over levels and fills the ponds and quenches the thirst of animals and people only after it has soaked the soil, so also, those who live in the truth can show kindness to others, but only after they have helped to meet the essential needs we all have.

The one who follows the way of love, not in word but in deed, cannot be mistaken in the direction in which he must apply his activity. One who devotes his life to the service of others will never be mistaken about the inutility of making bombs, of manufacturing elegant but useless objects, and of frittering away the hours of the day playing on the fiddle.

Love cannot be stupid. As love does not allow one to read a good novel to a person who is hungry and cold, so love does not allow one to live a life of amusement and comfort while the cold and hungry wither away from lack of necessities. True love — expressed in deeds, not words — not only cannot be stupid, but it alone supplies true sagacity and wisdom.

— *Essays, Letters, Miscellanies*

THE DEEDS OF LOVE

I think the best thing we can do to help the destitute is to live among them. This does not mean that we must all immediately go and freeze and starve ourselves to death or that anyone who fails to do this cannot do anything helpful. But the call of love is to love firsthand. The smallest of seeds can grow into the tallest of trees. So insignificant is what one, two, or a dozen people who live among the poorest can do, but it is to this we must give ourselves.

Some boys were leaving Moscow, where they had been working. One of them fell ill and was left behind by his companions. He had been waiting for five hours and was lying on the edge of the road, and a dozen peasants passed him by. One of them asked the sick lad some questions, and finding that he was ill took compassion on him and carried him to his home.

"Who is that?" "Whom has Akim brought home?"

The peasant explained that the boy was sick and that he had eaten nothing for two days — he could not help taking pity on him.

Then one woman brought some potatoes, another a meat patty, a third some milk.

"Akh! dear heart, he has been starving. Why, of course we will help him. He's only a boy!"

And this very lad, though wretched in appearance, and whom a dozen folks had passed by without taking pity on him, became the object of compassion, became dear, because one person had taken pity on him.

Deeds of love gain their power from the fact that they are contagious. Works of love expressed in heartfelt gifts of practical help give birth to the best sentiments: love and the eagerness to sacrifice.

Condescending deeds, like public assistance, however, breed nothing but resentment, both among the rich and the working class. "I have worked hard, I have struggled to get ahead, they give me nothing, but reward that lazy dog, that drunkard! Who told him to drink? He deserves all he gets!" exclaim those who refuse assistance.

The impoverished speak with no less resentment of the rich. "We are the poor ones. It is they who suck us dry! We not only can't get ahead, but can't get enough!"

Such feelings can only be overcome when we see one another, whoever we are, actually sharing with our neighbor, actually lending a personal hand to someone in need. In this lies the strength of loving activity. Its strength is that as soon as it becomes contagious, there is no limit to its spread.

As one candle kindles another, and thousands are lighted from that one, so also one heart inflames another and thousands

are set a-glowing. Millions of dollars will do less than the
smallest diminution of greediness or one heartfelt deed of compassion. When love — not "assistance" — is multiplied, then the
miracle of the loaves and fishes will occur once again. All will
be satisfied, with still more leftover.   — *What I Believe*

THE KEY TO THE GOSPELS

Of all the portions of the Gospels, the Sermon on the Mount
has exceptional importance. Nowhere does Jesus speak with
greater solemnity, nowhere does he offer moral guidance more
definitely and practically, nor do these words in any other form
awaken more readily an echo in the human heart. If there
are any clear and precise Christian principles, one can find
them here.

When I first approached these words I came away dis-
appointed. Jesus' words were not clear. They pointed to such
a far-reaching renunciation that they appeared to entirely stifle
life as I understood it: turn the other cheek, give up your cloak,
be at peace with everyone, love your enemies. How could such
renunciation lead to salvation?

To find help I read as many Bible commentaries on the
Gospels as I could get my hands on. But this was absolutely
fruitless. Everything Jesus said somehow was explained away.

I then recalled Jesus' words, "Except you . . . become as little
children, you shall not enter the kingdom of heaven" (Matt.
18:3), and it was then that I suddenly understood what had
been so confusing before. I understood what Jesus was saying,
not through exegetical leaps or profound and ingenious textual
maneuvers, but through a simple reading. And finally, it was
this passage that gave me the key to understanding: "You have
heard it said, 'An eye for an eye, and a tooth for a tooth.' But
I say to you, Do not resist evil."

The meaning of these words finally came to me; I understood that Jesus meant neither more nor less than what he said. What I saw was nothing new; only the veil that had hidden the truth from me fell away, and the truth was revealed in all its grandeur. These words suddenly appeared to me as if I had never read them before. I had never taken in that Jesus said, "Do not resist evil." It was as if these words had never existed or had never possessed a definite meaning.

Through a similar neglect of these words I had failed to understand what Jesus said directly afterward: "If someone strikes you on the right cheek, turn to him the other also...."

I thought to myself, "If I turn the other cheek, I shall get another blow. If I give to the one who asks, all that I have will be taken away. Life would become impossible. Surely Jesus couldn't have demanded this much. Surely he was using a figure of speech." But once I understood the words, "Do not resist evil," I saw that Jesus was not exaggerating one bit.

What did Jesus mean? "Do not resist evil, knowing that you will meet those who, when they have struck you on one cheek and are met with no resistance, will strike you on the other; who, having taken your coat, will take away your cloak also; who, having profited by your labor, will force you to labor still more without reward. And yet, though all this should happen to you, do not resist evil; do good to them that harm you."

When I understood these words as they were written, all that had been obscure became clear, and what had seemed exaggerated became perfectly reasonable. For the first time I grasped the pivotal point in the words, "Do not resist evil," and that what followed was only a clarification of this command. Jesus did not exhort us to turn the other cheek that we might endure suffering. His command was, "Do not resist evil," and he afterward declared suffering to be the probable consequence of putting this maxim into practice.

A father, when his son is about to set out on a far journey, commands him not to dally but to make haste. He does not tell him to pass his night without shelter, to deprive himself of food, to expose himself to rain and cold. He says, "Now go, don't wait, even though you will get wet and cold." So Jesus does not say, "Turn the other cheek and suffer." He says, "Do not resist evil. No matter what happens, do not resist."

These words were the key that opened for me all the rest of what Jesus commanded.

Whatever harm an evildoer may inflict upon you, bear it, give all that you have, and don't resist. Could anything be clearer, more definite, more intelligible than that? With these words, not only the Sermon on the Mount but the rest of the Gospels became clear to me. What had seemed contradictory was now in harmony. Above all, what had seemed superfluous was now indispensable. Each portion fell into unity and filled its proper part, like fragments of a broken statue when adjusted in harmony with the sculptor's design.

Everywhere Jesus pointed to this way of not resisting evil with evil. He who would not take up his cross, he who would not renounce worldly advantage, he who was not ready to bear all things for his sake, could not be his disciple. Jesus was clear. "Choose to be poor. Bear all without resistance to evil, even though you will thereby bring upon yourself persecution, suffering, and death. Prepare to suffer death rather than resist evil."

Jesus meant what he said. We may argue that such a command is difficult to put into practice. We may deny that he who follows it will find happiness. We may say that Jesus was a dreamer and idealist. But it is impossible not to admit that Jesus meant what he said. And what he said is the key that opens everything, but only if we push the key into the lock.

                                                        — *What I Believe*

THE NEW WAY

What should I do if I were to see a parent beating his child right before my eyes? I am not asking what my first impulse would be, but what I ought to do. If someone personally offends me my first impulse is to retaliate, but is this the right thing to do?

What is it actually that upsets me, what is it that I see as evil when a parent smacks his child? Is it the fact that the child gets hurt, or the fact that the parent is tormented by anger instead of being moved by love? Both. Evil involves estrangement between people. And so, if I am to act, I can only do so with the aim of destroying what separates, of restoring the relationship between the parent and the child.

But what should I do? Should I use violence against the parent? Most think this would be justified. Yet would this really restore a connection with the child? Or would it only serve to introduce yet a new wedge, a separation between the parent and me? So what am I to do? What about taking the place of the child oneself?

It is one thing to lay down one's life for one's brother in an act of defense, to expose oneself, to protect another with one's own chest, but to shoot someone in the name of trying to help is very different. Jesus' precept not to resist evil, not to repay evil for evil (Matt. 5:38–39) is the connecting link that brings together what has been broken. Nonresistant love alone destroys the germ of violence, which too often is carried out in the name of the good.

The way of nonresistance is easy to grasp, but difficult to accept. Our best lights tell us that it is true, but our heart rebels against it. Why is this?

Maybe we rebel because we think that Christ's teaching demands that we sit with our arms folded, gazing calmly at the evil that assaults our world. It is all very well for us, who are assured of life's necessities and are satisfied with enough to eat, or who are near the end of life, to chatter away and tell people that evil must be endured, but what about those who have nothing and who receive the brunt of the violence? If we are imbued with love for what is good and true, and with hatred for what is false and evil, then mustn't we dedicate our lives and make every step a battle against evil?

This sentiment is good, but it is precisely what led Peter to carry a knife and cut off the slave's ear. Imagine what would have happened if Jesus had not restrained his disciples. There would have been a brawl, and Jesus, not to mention his followers, would have been smashed. What then would have happened to Christ's teaching and mission?

Everyone readily admits that Christ taught us to love God and to love our neighbor as we love ourselves. But what or who is this God? What does love truly mean, especially when the object of one's love is an incomprehensible God? And who is my neighbor? What am I actually to do, especially in the face of evil?

At the very least, to love God means to love the truth, and to love one's neighbor as oneself means to acknowledge my solidarity with my neighbor. But even these words, which define very little, can be understood differently. How can one love God, whom each person understands in his or her own way and who some do not even acknowledge at all, and love one's neighbor as oneself, when one is imbued with a love for oneself that never leaves one for a moment, and often with an equally persistent hatred for others? This seems so unclear and impractical that it remains a mere phrase.

Herein lies the significance of Christ. He — his life and example — indicates how to fulfill God's will, which is the law of love, and the happiness that it affords. In the Sermon on the Mount, Christ lays down the simplest, easiest, most understandable laws for the expression of love toward God, toward one's neighbor, and toward life. To ignore these teachings, or to interpret them away into abstraction, is to abandon Christianity altogether.

We don't need to add anything to what Christ taught in order to discover the kingdom of truth. In fact, the following commands, the essence of Christ's teaching, are enough to know the way: (1) Do not be angry; (2) Do not commit fornication; (3) Do not swear oaths; (4) Do not go to law; (5) Do not go to war.

Christ's teaching embraces our entire lives, individually and of humanity as a whole. And if we take his commands separately and apply them directly to ourselves, we would experience the unimaginably blessed result that he promises. His commands are not only easy but even pleasant to fulfill.

What if only a fraction of the efforts devoted by people to overcoming evil through force were devoted instead to enduring evil, refusing to participate in it, and continuing to shine with the light that has been given to each one of us?

What if, for example, one, two, dozens, or hundreds of youth were simply to say when they are called up for military service: "We cannot be murderers since we follow Christ — the Christ you good Christian people even profess." What would result I don't know, but I do know that it would bring about progress.

"But," people say to me, "if you believe that there can be no genuinely human life without fulfilling Christ's words, and if you love the life you preach, why then do you not carry out all of Christ's precepts?"

I admit that I am guilty, and vile, and worthy of contempt for failing to fully carry out Christ's teaching. At the same time, not to justify myself, but simply to explain my lack of consistency, I say: "Look at my life now and compare it to my former life. You will see that I am trying to live out the truth I proclaim. True, I have not fulfilled a fraction of Christ's will, and I am ashamed of this, but I have failed to fulfill his Word not because I do not wish to, but because I have been unable to. Teach me how to escape from the net of temptations that surrounds me, help me, and I will fulfill Christ's teachings. Even without help I wish and hope to fulfill them. Attack me, I do this myself, but attack *me* rather than the path I follow, which I point out to anyone who asks me where I think it lies. If I know the way home and am walking along it drunkenly, is it any less the right way simply because I am staggering from side to side?

"If it is not the right way, then show me another way. But if I stagger and lose the way, you must help me and keep me on the true path, just as I am ready to support you. Do not mislead me, do not be glad that I have gotten lost, do not gleefully shout, 'Look at him! He said he was going home, but there he is crawling into a bog!' No, do not gloat, but give me your help and support. For you are not devils in the swamp, but people like me who are seeking the way home. For I am alone and it cannot be that I wish to go into the swamp. Help me, my heart is breaking in despair that we have all lost our way."

So this is my attitude to Christ's teaching. I try to fulfill it with all I've got. I not only repent for each failure, but also beg for help in fulfilling it. And I joyfully welcome anyone who, like me, is looking for the path; and I listen to him.

— Essays and Letters

NOTES FOR SOLDIERS

You are a soldier. You have been taught to shoot, to stab, to march, to train, to obey. It has not even entered your head to ask yourself whether what you have been ordered to do is good or bad. But suddenly an order is received that your company or squadron shall march out, taking heavy ammunition. You go without asking where you are going.

You are brought to a village or factory, and you see before you in an open space a crowd of people — men, women with children, elderly. Some officials, along with policemen, approach the crowd. At first, the crowd is quiet, but then it begins to shout louder and louder, and the authorities retreat. And you conclude that a riot is about to occur and that you have been brought in to "pacify" the crowd. The shouting grows louder and louder, and you are then given an order to prepare to shoot.

You are ordered to first shoot above the heads of the crowd. But the crowd does not disperse, and shouts even louder. So you are ordered to shoot in earnest, not over the heads, but straight into the middle of the crowd.

You've been told that you are not responsible for the consequences of your actions. Yet you know that *you* and no one else have killed the person who falls bleeding from your shot, and you know that you could have refrained from shooting and that this person would not have been killed.

What are you to do?

It would not be enough to lay down your arms and refuse in this instance to shoot your brothers, for tomorrow the same thing will reoccur. And therefore, whether you want to or not, you have to stop and think and ask, "What is this soldier's calling that has brought me to the point of shooting my unarmed fellow human beings?"

You recall what is said in the Bible: "You shall not kill." You remember what Jesus told his disciples: "Do not be angry with your brother, do not hate your enemies, but love them...." And yet those in authority tell you that in war, and in your duty as a soldier, things are different. In situations of conflict it is not a sin to kill. And because you have taken an oath, you must at times kill, and thus not you but your commanders will be responsible for your actions.

But then you also remember what is said in the Gospel: "Swear not at all...." Taking the oath is a sin. And immediately you realize you are answerable to your conscience, not to your sergeant, captain, or someone else. You know that *you* must decide what you can and must do, and what you cannot and should not do. You are always responsible for what you do.

We are responsible before God for our actions. No power on earth has the right to turn a living person into a dead thing, into a mere instrument, which one can move about as one likes. Christ taught us that we are children of God. How then can we ever give over our conscience into the power of another person?

Be assured that those who have assumed power over your life, demanding of you that you kill upon command, are deceivers, or are themselves caught in a web of deception. These are the very ones you must not obey.

— *Writings on Civil Disobedience*

DO UNTO OTHERS

Let us suppose that a brigand is raising his knife over his victim. I see him and am armed with a revolver, so I could kill him. But I am not absolutely sure what the brigand will do. He might not strike, while I would surely kill him. That is why the only thing one can do in such as case, as in all other similar cases, is to follow an invariable rule of conduct dictated by conscience. And conscience may demand the loss of one's own life, but never that of another's.

None of us can foresee the future, but all of us can act according to the golden rule: Do unto others as you would have them do unto you.

"But others steal, pillage, kill, while I do none of these things. Let them follow the law of mutual help, then I too will be willing to observe it." So objects the common person, and with greater certainty the higher up he or she is on the social ladder.

"I do not steal," says the king, the president, the general, the judge, the estate holder, the businessman, the soldier, the policeman. But in fact, our very social order depends on violence. It's just that we fail to see all the crimes committed each day, all in the name of the public good. Instead, we see only the rare, vulgar forms of violence and concern ourselves only with those who are *called* murderers and thieves.

"He is a murderer, he is a thief. He does not observe the rule of not doing unto others what you would not have them do unto you," say the very same people who kill in war, force entire nations to prepare for carnage, and steal from and pillage their own as well as foreign countries in the name of free enterprise. If the rule of mutual help has no more effect upon those who in our society are deemed murderers or thieves, it is only because they constitute a part of the vast majority of people who for generation upon generation have been robbed and despoiled by those who do not see the criminal character of their own acts.

"How could we do otherwise than resist the invasion of our country by savages who come to take away our property, our wives and daughters?" object those who wish to protect themselves from the same crimes that they commit against other nations. "Yellow peril," shout out the whites. "White peril," cry, with more justification, the Indians, Chinese, and Japanese.

But as soon as we become free of the myths that seek to justify violence, we readily understand all the horror of the crimes committed by one nation against another. Even more, we grasp the moral stupidity that incites "free nations" to dream of protecting themselves against the very acts of violence that they commit elsewhere.

It should be enough to see how futile it is to engage in violence on the basis of what we think we can know of the future. This is only guesswork used to justify violence and our present system. But if this isn't enough, then we should be able to understand well enough how the need to oppose evil by violence is little more that our way of justifying our own habitual vices of vengeance, cupidity, envy, ambition, pride, cowardice, and spite.

— *The Law of Love and the Law of Violence*

IS THIS HUMAN NATURE?

We have only to examine closely the complicated mechanism of our institutions that are based upon coercion to realize that coercion and violence are fundamentally contrary to human nature. The judge, who has condemned according to the law, is not willing to hang the criminal with his own hands. No clerk would tear a villager from his weeping family and cast him into prison. The general or the soldier, unless he be hardened by discipline and service, will not undertake to slay a hundred Turks or Germans or destroy a village, would not, if he could help it, directly kill a single person. Yet all these things are done, thanks to the administrative machinery that divides responsibility for misdeeds in such a way that no one feels them to be contrary to nature.

What is the law of human nature? Does my security and that of my family, do all my amusements and pleasures, have to be purchased at the expense of misery, deprivation, and suffering to thousands of human beings — by the terror of death chambers, by the misfortune of thousands stifling within prison walls, by the fear inspirited by millions of soldiers and guardians of civilization, torn from their homes and scarred by inhuman discipline, to protect our pleasures with loaded guns against the possible interferences of desperate intruders? Does my well-being, does every fragment of bread that I put in my mouth and the mouths of my children really have to depend on countless privations? Or can this piece of bread belong to me because I know that everyone else has a share, and that no one starves while I eat?

Once we grasp the fact that, due to our social organization, each one of our pleasures, every minute of our cherished tranquility, is obtained at the expense of others' suffering, we will come to understand what is natural and what is not. It is we — all of us — who pull the trigger.   — *What I Believe*

WHO IS SUFFERING?

Try and remember all the painful moments in your life, all the physical and spiritual pain you have endured and perhaps still suffer. Ask yourself: Wherein lies your suffering? What gives rise to it? Are you suffering for the sake of the truth, because you are seeking to follow Christ and his teaching? Or is your situation on account of trying to follow the ways and wisdom of this world?

In my own life, which has been exceptionally fortunate in a worldly sense, I have suffered plenty. The worst moments of my life, however, were due to the drunkenness and debauchery of student days, duels, war, and so on, to that poor health and those unnatural and difficult conditions of life in which I now live — all this "martyrdom" is on account of my striving after worldly values.

People think that this kind of suffering is normal, even unavoidable. Happiness in this world comes with a price, so people say. And so we assure ourselves that all our misfortunes, including those we inflict upon ourselves, are necessary conditions of life. In all this we are unable to see the wisdom of Christ's teaching and the happiness promised to us if we would but follow it: "Whoever wants to save his life must lose it, but whoever loses his life for me will save it" (Luke 9:24).

So where is true happiness to be found, people ask. Look at any large crowd of people, especially those who are relatively well off. Note their wearied, distressed, sickly faces. Where is the light in their eyes? Think about those you know and those you've read about. Consider all the violent deaths, all the suicides, all the loneliness, and ask yourself for whose sake is all this suffering, despair, and death? Aren't most of these tragedies unnecessary — ones we bring on ourselves?

Now think about the vast millions who struggle to survive, who barely have enough. Thousands leave their homes, fields, families and abandon everything, even their very lives, and flock to the cities all to acquire the world's happiness. And they all — not to mention those tens of thousands of unfortunate people who have lost everything and struggle along on garbage and vodka in the doss houses — they all, from the factory hands, cabmen, seamstresses, and prostitutes, to the rich merchants and ministers of state with their wives, endure the most trying and unnatural manner of life and yet fail to obtain what is supposed to bring them happiness.

Whether poor or rich, everyone is running after things they don't really need but are supposed to make them happy. As soon as we get what it is we're supposed to have, we desire something else, and again something else, and so the work of Sisyphus goes on and on, leading to an empty, miserable life. Today I purchase a new suit, tomorrow a watch and chain, then carpets in the living room, then race-horses and art work in gilt frames, until finally I fall ill from my frantic labors and die. Another continues the same labor, and also sacrifices his life to that same Moloch; he too dies and also does not know why he did what he did. Is this happiness?

It might be plausible to believe that the fulfillment of Christ's teaching is too difficult and leads to too many hardships if it were the case that chasing after the world's prize were easy, safe, and pleasant. But in fact what society deems worthy is far more dangerous and tormenting than trying to live according to the pattern of Christ.

Count up all the "martyrs," and for each Christian martyr you will find a thousand worldly martyrs whose sufferings are a hundred times more terrible. Those slain in war alone should be enough to make us see that Christ's way is far more beneficial. These soldiers, not to mention all the innocent civilians, were all martyrs to the world's philosophy of power and prosperity. They didn't even have to follow Christ's teachings but only abstain from violence in order to have escaped from this kind of suffering and death.

Countless people suffer on account of taking up the cause of war; thousands of millions more are pinned to a life of drudgery for the sake of worldly success. But those who suffer on account of the truth, it is they who have life; they are the ones who are "alive" and at peace.

Christ calls us to a spring of water that is right beside us. People are tormented by thirst, eat dirt, drink one another's blood, but then they are told that to go to the spring to which Christ directs them involves too great a sacrifice. And people believe this. But they suffer and die of thirst, being only two steps from the living water, not daring to go to it.

Christ did not call us to sacrifice anything. On the contrary, he warns against the deception of riches so as to point us to what is better for us here and now. We'll be happy only when we forgo our possessions; we'll be blessed once we stop trying to overcome evil with evil. He teaches us that we must at all times be prepared to die, for we cannot be sure of a single hour of life. And we imagine all this to be a terrible sacrifice! No. It is only a declaration of the conditions in which each of us must inevitably live.

We are so used to the pretense that everything we create for the imaginary security of our life — our armies, military bases, stores, clothes, and hospitals, our property and our money — seems really necessary for life. For whatever the reason, we believe the lie that we can secure for ourselves a life free of suffering and strife. We are so caught up in this lie that we fail to notice all we lose by it. And we lose everything — our whole life. We become so absorbed in safeguarding our lives that no life is left in us.

Our life is never secure. And in our effort to make it so we ruin the very thing we wish to secure. Armies mobilize to protect what is ours, but in doing this hundreds of thousands of lives are lost. The rich secure their lives by obtaining more and more money, but it is this very money that attracts the robber who kills them. An anxiety-ridden man tries to make his life better by undergoing a cure, but the medicine itself slowly deprives him of life, like that sick man who sat thirty-eight years at the pool waiting for the angel of healing to come (John 5:2–8).

Which way — Christ or the world's — leads to suffering? Let us think again before we dismiss what Jesus commands in favor of the world's wisdom. For he alone has the words of eternal life. He is the Way, the Truth, and the Life.

— What I Believe

WHAT'S THE GOVERNMENT TO DO?

Every government knows how to defend itself from revolutionaries, and has resources for doing so. But what are governments to do against those who show the uselessness, superfluousness, and perniciousness of all governments, and who do not contend against them, but simply do not need them and do without them, and therefore are unwilling to take any part in them?

Revolutionaries and activists assert that the system is bad, that we must overturn it and substitute something new. The Christian says, I know nothing about the government or the "system," I don't know ultimately whether it is good or bad, and I don't want to overturn it, precisely because I don't know whether it is good or bad; but for the very same reason I don't want to support it either. And I not only don't want to, but I can't, because what it demands of me is against my conscience.

Revolutionaries attack the government from without. Christianity does not attack it at all, but, from within it destroys all the foundations on which government rests. It does so precisely because the Christian is free from subjecting himself to all forms of coercion. For this reason, the Christian refuses to pay taxes that are directly spent on deeds of violence — on the pay of men of violence — soldiers, on the construction of prisons, fortresses, and artillery. They regard it as sinful and immoral to have any hand in such deeds.

All power arrangements, such as the state, are against the conscience of a Christian — the oath of allegiance, taxes, law proceedings, and military service. The whole power of the government rests on these very obligations.

Those who refuse to take the oath of allegiance refuse because to promise obedience to authorities, that is, to those who rely on deeds of violence, is contrary to Christ's teaching. They refuse to take the oath in the law courts, because Christ commands them not to. They refuse to perform police duties, because in the performance of these duties they must use force, and a Christian cannot do that. They refuse to take part in trials at law, because they consider every appeal to law as fulfilling the law of vengeance, which is inconsistent with the Christian law of forgiveness and love. They refuse to take any part in military preparations and in the army, because they cannot be executioners, and they are unwilling to prepare themselves to be so.

The motives in all these cases are so virtuous that even the most oppressive governments can hardly punish them openly. To punish people for refusing to act against their conscience the government must renounce all claim to good sense and benevolence. And they assure people that they only rule in the name of good sense and benevolence.

What are governments to do against such people?

Governments can of course flog to death or execute or keep in perpetual imprisonment all enemies who want to overturn them by violence; they can lavish gold on that section of the people who are ready to destroy their enemies. But what can they do against those who, without wishing to overturn or destroy anything, desire simply for their part to do nothing against the law of Christ, and who, therefore, refuse to perform the most common state requirements, which are, therefore, the most indispensable to the maintenance of the state?

What is to be done with people who profess no revolutionary ideas nor any peculiar religious dogmas, but merely are unwilling to kill anyone, refuse to take the oath, to pay taxes, to take part in law proceedings, to serve in the army, to fulfill, in fact, any of the obligations upon which the whole fabric of a state rests? What is to done with such people? To buy them over with bribes is impossible; the very risks to which they voluntarily expose themselves show that they cannot compromise. To dupe them into believing that submission to those in authority is their duty to God is also impossible, since their refusal is based on the clear, unmistakable Gospel, recognized even by those who are trying to compel others to act against it.

To terrify them by threats is still less possible, because the deprivations and sufferings to which they are subjected only strengthen their desire to follow the faith by which they are commanded to obey God rather than men, and not to fear those who can destroy the body, but to fear him who can destroy body and soul. To kill them or to confine them in prison is also impossible. These people have friends, and their way of thinking and acting is well known. They are known to be upright, gentle, peaceable people. How then can they be regarded as criminals who must be removed for the safety of society? And to put these people to death would only provoke others to champion them and their cause.

The Christian of conscience puts the ruling powers into a desperate position. Already ruling governments feel their weak and defenseless position, and people of Christian principles are awakening from their apathy, and already begin to feel their power. "I have come to bring fire on the earth," said Christ, "and how I wish it were already kindled?" And this fire is beginning to burn.   *— The Kingdom of God Is within You*

IS THE STATE NECESSARY?

The champions of government argue that without the state the wicked will oppress and outrage the good, and that only the power of the government enables the good to resist the wicked. Those who argue thus take it for granted that the good are those who are in possession of power, and the bad are those who are in subjection to it. But this is just what begs to be proved. Nor does it occur to them that those who are genuinely "good" cannot seize power, nor retain it. To do so indicates a love of power, and love of power is inconsistent with goodness; but quite consistent with pride, cunning, and cruelty.

Much of history is nothing but a recital of the incidents and means by which the more wicked gain power over the less wicked, and how they retain power by coercion and deception. History clearly shows how those in power rule under the pretense of guarding the right and protecting the good from the wicked. The revolutions in history are only examples of how this all gets played out, the more wicked seizing power and oppressing the good in the name of guarding the right.

What is ironic is the fact that all the arguments brought forward by those in authority in their own defense can with even tighter logic be advanced against them. They plead the danger of violence — most often imagined in the future — but they are all the while practicing violence themselves.

Consider what the oppressed can say to their oppressors. "You say that people used to pillage and murder in the past, and that you are afraid that they will pillage and murder one another if your power were no more. That may happen — or it may not happen. But the fact that you ruin thousands of people in prisons, break up millions of families and ruin millions of people, physically as well as morally, in the military, that fact is not an imaginary but a real act of violence, which, according to your own argument, you ought to oppose by violence. And so you are yourselves the oppressors against whom, according to your own argument, it is necessary to use violence."

State-sanctioned violence is nothing but a ploy. In arguing that the use of force is necessary in order to protect the public good, the ruling authorities only show their disinclination to let other oppressors come to power who would like to snatch it from them. But in asserting this they only accuse themselves, saying that their power is needed to defend us from other possible oppressors in the present or in the future.

— *The Kingdom of God Is within You*

3

Prophetic Forays

THE DESTRUCTION OF HELL
AND ITS RESTORATION: A LEGEND

This happened when Christ came to this earth to reveal his will. His teaching was so clear, so easy to follow, and so power-fully freed people from evil that it was all but impossible not to accept it. Nothing could stop it from spreading.

Beelzebub, the father and ruler of all the devils, was trou-bled. He could clearly see that unless Christ stopped preaching, his own power would be ended forever. He was quite anxious, but instead of falling into despair he encouraged his servants, the scribes and Pharisees, to insult and torment Christ for all they were worth. At the same time he urged Christ's disciples to abandon Jesus. He hoped that, after being sentenced to a shameful death, after being reviled, after being abandoned by all his disciples, and after undergoing the agony of crucifixion itself, Christ would at the last moment renounce his teaching. Then his message would be destroyed.

But it was on the cross that all this was decided. When Christ exclaimed, "My God, my God, why have you forsaken me?" Beelzebub exulted. He seized the fetters that had been prepared, put them on his own legs and adjusted them so that once they had been put on the legs of Christ they could never again be undone.

But then came the words, "Father, forgive them, for they know not what they do," and, "It is finished."

Beelzebub realized instantly that all was lost. He wanted to remove the fetters from his legs, but was unable to move. The fetters were welded onto him, binding his legs. He wanted to use his wings to fly, but was unable to open them. Then Beelzebub saw Christ at the gates of Hell, surrounded by a halo of light. He saw how all the sinners, from Adam to Judas, came out, how the devils ran off in all directions, how the walls of Hell silently collapsed on all four sides. Unable to bear all this, he let out a piercing shriek and disappeared through the gaping floor of Hell into the lower regions.

•

A hundred years passed by, two hundred, three hundred.

Beelzebub did not count the time. He lay in the lower regions without moving, surrounded by black gloom and deathly silence, trying not to think about what had happened. Unable not to think about it, he was filled with impotent hatred for the one who had brought about his ruin.

But suddenly — he had no idea how many hundred years had passed — he heard above him something that sounded like the tramping of feet, groans, cries, and the gnashing of teeth.

Beelzebub lifted up his head a little and began to listen.

That Hell could be restored was more than he could believe. But he could definitely hear the trampling, the groans, the cries, and the gnashing of teeth, and all the more clearly.

Beelzebub raised himself up, doubled up his shaggy legs with their unkempt hooves (his fetters, to his amazement, had dropped off all by themselves), opened out his wings, flapped them, and gave the whistle by which in former times he had called his servants and helpers.

He had barely drawn his breath when an opening appeared above his head. There was a flash of red flame, and a crowd of devils, crushing against one another, dropped out of the opening into the lower regions. They settled in a circle around Beelzebub like crows around carrion.

There were big devils and little devils, fat devils and thin devils, devils with long tails and devils with short tails, devils with pointed horns, devils with crooked horns, and devils with straight horns.

One of them, a shiny black devil who was quite naked except for a cape thrown over his shoulders, with a round, hairless face and a vast, dropping paunch, was squatting right in front of Beelzebub. He was rolling his flaming eyes up and down, waving his long, thin tail rhythmically from side to side, and smiling, continually smiling.

"What does all that noise mean?" asked Beelzebub, pointing up above. "What's going on?"

"The same thing is happening as before," answered the shiny devil in the cape.

"So there really are sinners?" asked Beelzebub.

"Lots of them," replied the shiny devil.

"And what about the teaching of the man I prefer not to name?" asked Beelzebub.

The devil in the cape bared his sharp teeth in a grin while the other devils let out suppressed laughs.

"His teaching doesn't bother us. They don't believe it," said the devil with the cape.

"But his teaching all too clearly delivers them from us, from sin and evil. He bore witness to it with his own death on the cross," said Beelzebub.

"I altered it," replied the devil in the cape, tapping his tail rapidly against the floor.

"How?"

"In a way where people believe not in his teaching, but in mine, which they call by his name."

"How in the world did you do that?" exclaimed Beelzebub.

"It happened by itself. I just helped."

"Go on. Tell me more," said Beelzebub.

The devil in the cape lowered his head and fell silent for a while as though lost in thought. Then he began.

"After those terrible events, after Hell had been destroyed and our father and ruler had left us, I went to visit the places where the teaching that so nearly ruined us had been spread. I wanted to see the life of the people who followed it. I soon realized that they were entirely happy and quite beyond our grasp. They never stayed angry with one another, they didn't succumb to the charms of vanity, and they either kept to one wife or didn't marry at all. They held everything in common and owned no property, they didn't use force to defend themselves, and they repaid evil not with evil but with good. Their life was so excellent that more and more people came to them. I thought indeed that everything was lost and I almost left. But then something happened, something quite insignificant in itself but which seemed worth my attention. And so I remained.

"Some of these people thought that everyone who came to them should be circumcised, and that one should not eat food that had been offered to idols. Others believed differently, that circumcision was quite unnecessary, and that it was perfectly fine to eat whatever was placed before you. I began to suggest to both sides that this disagreement was vitally important and that it was imperative that no one give in. They believed me, and their arguments grew more bitter and complicated. Each became convinced that they were the sole possessors of the truth....

"Things were going well, but I was afraid that they might see through this rather obvious deception. So I eventually thought up the idea of a "church," a structure with authority to decide. Once they fell for that, I felt assured. I knew that we were saved and that Hell was restored."

•

"What in hell, or should I say on earth, is the 'church'?" asked Beelzebub severely, reluctant to believe that his servants could be cleverer than he was himself.

"Well, when people compromise and know that no one believes them, they always call on God, saying, 'By God, what I say is the truth!' Well, this in short is the church, except that the people who call themselves the church really believe they can never be wrong. And so, whatever nonsense they come out with, they can never take back. These people look on themselves as possessors of the truth, not because what they preach is true, but because they think they alone are the legitimate heirs of the disciples of the disciples of the disciples of the disciples of the Teacher. Although this method of deception has the disadvantage where different and opposing people each claim to be part of the true church, it does prevent these same people from being able to take back anything they say, however absurd it may be and whatever other people may say."

"But what made the church misinterpret so badly the teachings of its Master?" asked Beelzebub.

"Once they announced themselves as the sole possessors of the truth, and once they convinced the people that *they* were the supreme judges of their fates, they obtained supreme power. With this they naturally grew arrogant, and in most cases depraved, and so aroused the people's indignation and enmity. Having no other weapons against their enemies except force, they took to persecuting, executing, and burning anyone who did not agree with them. The very position they had taken up forced them, in turn, to further misinterpret the teaching in order to justify their evil ways and the cruel methods they employed against their enemies. And that is just what they did."

•

"But the teaching was so simple and so clear," uttered Beelzebub, still not wanting to believe that his servants could have done something he had never even thought of himself. Who could possibly misinterpret, "Do unto others as you would have them do unto you"!

"On my advice," replied the devil in the cape, "a number of different methods were used. Humans have a story about a good magician who turned a man into a grain of millet in order to save him from an evil magician. The evil magician turned himself into a cock and was about to peck up the grain when the good magician emptied out a whole sack of other grain. The evil magician was unable to eat up all the grain, nor could he find the one grain he wanted. The same thing was done, on my advice, with the command to do unto others what you would want them to do to you. Piles of officially recognized theological works — a heap of false and half truths — were dumped on this one simple and incomprehensible truth, thus making it impossible to find the one truth that they really needed.

"The second method, used with great success for over a thousand years, was simply to coerce or kill or burn anyone who wanted to give witness to the real truth. Although this method has, by and large, gone out of use, it has not been entirely abandoned. Although they no longer burn or torture people, they poison their lives, slandering and shunning them so fiercely that only a few people dare to stand up to them.

"The third method is as follows. Since the church claims to have the authority, its leaders deem themselves in some way or another as infallible. In this way they are able to teach the opposite of what has been written in the Scriptures, leaving their members to find their own way out of these contradictions. For example, the Teacher said: 'Call no one father upon the earth: for one is your Father, which is in Heaven. Neither let yourselves be called masters: for one is your master, the Christ' (Matt. 23:9–10). In spite of this, these people say: 'We alone are fathers and we alone are masters.' Again, it is written: 'When you pray, do so in secret, and God will hear you' (Matt. 6:6). They, however, teach the people to pray in church buildings, all together, with singing and music. It is written: 'Swear not at all.'

They, to the contrary, teach the people how they must bow to the authorities and submit to their demands. It is written: 'Do not kill.' They, however, explain that one can and must kill during wars and executions. It is written: 'My word is spirit and life. Feed upon it as upon bread.' But they teach that if you dip pieces of bread in wine and say certain words over them, then the bread and the wine will save your soul. The people believe all this and diligently eat their sops; they are astonished when they end up with us to find that these sops have been of no help whatsoever."

The devil in the cape came to an end, rolling his eyes and grinning from ear to ear.

"All this is excellent," smiled Beelzebub. The devils all burst into loud laughter.

•

"So do you really have fornicators, robbers, and murderers, just like before?" asked Beelzebub, now speaking quite gaily.

The devils, also growing more animated, began talking all at once, each of them trying to show off in front of Beelzebub.

"No, not like before!" shouted one devil. "There are more of them than before, and better disguised!"

"There isn't enough room in the old part for all the adulterers," squealed another.

"And robbers now are much worse than they used to be," shouted a third.

"We can't get enough fuel for all the murderers," bellowed a fourth.

"Don't all talk at once! I want the one I question to reply, and no one else. Whoever is in charge of immorality, come forward and tell me what you do with those whom the Teacher forbade to divorce or even look on another with lust. Who is in charge of immorality?"

"I am," replied an effeminate brown devil, as he shuffled toward Beelzebub on his bottom. He had a flabby face and slobbering jaws that were constantly in motion. He squatted in front of the other devils, bent his head to one side, tucked his tufted tail between his legs, waved it about, and began in a sing-song voice:

"We use both the old way, the way that you, our father and ruler, used in Paradise in order to deliver the whole human race into our hands, and a new ecclesiastical, religious way. Let me tell about this new way. We convince people, for example, that marriage is not a matter of faithful love, but a matter of getting dressed in one's finest clothes, going into a beautifully decorated building for the occasion, putting on special hats and dancing certain steps to the accompaniment of various songs. We make people believe that this is what constitutes a marriage. Sexual pleasure outside marriage is thus viewed as something involving no special obligations."

The effeminate devil bent his head to the other side and fell silent, as though waiting for Beelzebub's reaction.

Beelzebub nodded his head in approval and the devil continued. "It is by this method, not forgetting the earlier method employed in Paradise, that of curiosity and the forbidden fruit," he continued, obviously hoping to flatter Beelzebub, "that we achieve our finest successes. Under the illusion that they can arrange an honest church wedding for themselves, even after they have engaged a number of different partners, people feel it quite natural to leave their spouses — one after the other. If they feel constrained by some of the requirements of a church marriage, then they arrange to dance a few more steps, the first steps being proclaimed invalid."

The effeminate devil fell silent. Wiping his slobbering mouth with the end of his tail, he bent his head to the other side and stared at Beelzebub.

•

"Very simple and very good," responded Beelzebub. "You have my approval. And who is in charge of stealing?"

"I am." A large devil came forward, with big, crooked horns, a moustache that pointed upward, and huge, equally crooked paws. He crawled to the front like the other one and arranged his moustache military fashion with both paws, waiting to be questioned.

"The one who destroyed Hell," said Beelzebub, "taught the people to live like the birds of the air, saying that one must give one's coat to anyone who demands one's shirt, and that one must give away everything he had in order to enter the kingdom. How do you hoodwink people who have heard that into committing robbery?"

"We do it," replied the devil with the moustache, throwing his head back loftily, "in the same way our father and ruler did when Saul became king. We make people think, just as you did then, that instead of everyone deciding not to steal from one another it would be easier if they all allowed themselves to be robbed by some absolute power — one with supreme authority. The only novelty in our method is our way of authorizing this power to steal. With regards to the church (for we have different methods we use for the state), a special hat is placed on the authority's head. He then sits on a tall chair, with a stick and ball in his hands, smeared with vegetable oil, and then it is proclaimed, in the name of God, that his person and position is sacred. With that there are virtually no restrictions on the amount that he can take.

"These sacred persons, together with their assistants and their assistants' assistants, quietly plunder the people, not incurring the least danger. At the same time they support laws and regulations that allow an idle minority to steal from the laboring majority without fear of punishment. Some states have recently come to allow this robbery to continue in exactly the same way, but without anyone being anointed. As our father and ruler can see, the method we use is essentially the same one that has always been used. All that is different is that we have made it more general, more hidden, more universal in time and space, and also more stable.

"The way we have made it more general is as follows. Previously people submitted to a person they had chosen themselves. We, however, have arranged things so that they submit to anyone, as long as they follow the law.

"We have made it more hidden in that the people who are robbed, thanks to the system of indirect taxation, no longer see anything of their robbers. And with the system of public and state loans, it is not only the living who are robbed, but also the generations to come.

"The method is more universal in that the so-called Christians, not completely happy with robbing their own people, rob foreigners. This they carry out under the strangest of pretexts, mainly that of propagating Christianity.

"This whole approach is more stable insofar as the chief robbers and their institutions are considered, if not sacred, necessary. No one dares to oppose them.... And so nowadays open robbery — taking someone's purse, horse, or clothes — constitutes barely a millionth part of the legitimate robberies that are carried out every day by those who have the power. Nowadays the practice and means of stealing has become so well entrenched in society that it has become the main activity of nearly everyone, moderated only by conflicts between the robbers themselves."

•

"Well, that is quite clever," affirmed Beelzebub. "But what about murder? Who is in charge of murder?"

"I am," answered a blood-red devil as he slithered out from the crowd. He had fangs that stuck out from his mouth, pointed horns, and a thick tail that pointed upward without moving.

"How do you make murderers out of the disciples of the one who said: 'Do not return evil for evil, but love your enemies?' What do you do to turn them into murderers?"

"We use the old method," answered the red devil in a deafening voice, "of exciting avarice, discord, hatred, vengeance, and pride. And we still persuade the teachers of men that the best way for them to deter others from murder is publicly to murder all murderers. This notion, however, serves not so much to turn people into killers as to prepare them for it.

"You wonder what has given us the largest number of murders? The authority of the church has been a help. But nowadays it is quite often the teaching of equality that brings about murder. According to this idea, all people are equal before the law. People who have been robbed, however, feel that this is not the case. As they see it, this "equality" only makes it easier for the robbers to continue to rob, while making it difficult for them to do the same. As a result, they indignantly attack their plunderers, justifying themselves on the basis of law. And then comes mutual murder — in the name of revolution and counter-revolution — something that can lead to tens of thousands of murderers all at once."

"But what about war?" inquired Beelzebub. "How do you entice people to war when they've been taught to love their enemies, being they are all children of one father?"

The red devil grinned, letting out a stream of fire and smoke from his mouth, and joyfully slapping himself on the back with his thick tail.

"This is what we do. We persuade each side that its ideals and its interests are actually in the interest and betterment of the entire world, and as such it is their duty to lead the way and demonstrate their superiority over others. Since they have all been imbued with the same rationale, they all think they are in danger from their neighbors. Thus they make constant and more destructive preparations for self-defense. And the more one country prepares to defend itself against those it hates, the more these enemies do the same. And Presto! The people either preoccupy themselves with preparing for war or in waging it."

•

"Now, that is intelligent," muttered Beelzebub after a short silence. "But how is it that the scholars aren't able to see through all this deception? Why haven't they reestablished the truth?"

"Because they are unable to," replied a matte-black devil in a self-assured voice. He crawled forward, dressed in a mantle. He had a flat, sloping forehead, large protruding ears, and etiolated limbs.

"Why is that?" asked Beelzebub sternly, irritated by the devil's self-assured tone of voice.

Not in the least embarrassed by Beelzebub's question, the devil in the mantle calmly sat down in the oriental fashion, crossing his puny legs instead of squatting as the others had done. Without the least hesitation he began to speak in a quiet, measured tone of voice.

"They are unable to reestablish the truth because I divert their attention from what they can know and need to know to what they do not need to know and can never know."

"And how do you do that?"

"I use different techniques at different times. Long ago I got them to argue about various details regarding the relationship between the three persons of the Trinity, about the origin and nature of Christ, about the attributes of God, and so on. They debated all this at great length, arguing, quarreling, and growing angry with one another. They became so obsessed with these discussions that they failed to examine how they and others actually lived their lives. As a result they no longer needed to know what their teacher taught them about how to live.

"Later on, when they had grown so confused in their arguments that they no longer had any idea what they were talking about, I persuaded some people that what mattered most was to study and explicate what was written thousands of years ago — especially by a Greek named Aristotle. I then convinced others that what really mattered was to find a stone they could use to make gold, and also an elixir that would heal their illnesses and make the people immortal. And so the most intelligent and learned men devoted all their intellectual powers to these questions.

"I persuaded other people, those not interested in these questions, to concern themselves with whether the earth spins around the sun, or the sun around the earth. When they discovered that it was the earth that moved and not the sun, and had worked out how many millions of miles it was from the earth to the sun, they felt extremely pleased with themselves indeed. Since then they have been studying the distances between the stars with even greater diligence, although they are perfectly aware that there is no end to these distances, and that the number of stars is countless.

"I also made people think it was vital to find out the exact origin of all the animals, all the worms, all the plants, and all the tiniest creatures. And although it is clearly equally unnecessary to find out such things, they still devote all their intellectual powers to such investigations of material phenomena, constantly expressing astonishment that the more unnecessary things they learn, the more there is to learn. What remains to be studied, therefore, happens to expand, and the more complex the objects of study become, the more irrelevant their knowledge becomes with regards to life. Although this is obvious, it doesn't seem to worry them in the least. Convinced of the importance of their activities, they keep on researching, teaching, writing, publishing, and translating debates and investigations that for the most part have no practical value. And if on occasion their activities do have a practical application, it tends to increase the comfort of the rich minority or to aggravate the condition of the poor.

"To prevent the people from ever guessing that the one thing they need most is to understand how to live according to the teachings of Christ, I persuade them that the laws of life of the soul are unknowable, that moral and religious ideas are intellectually meaningless. How to live is best determined by sociology, a science I have thought up myself, and whose object is to study the various bad ways of life led in the past. As a result, instead of following the simple teachings of Christ, they think it wisest to consider how others have lived, and then deduce various general laws of life from these lives.

"To get them still deeper into error, I convince them that the tradition of science and all that it asserts is the only proper ground for knowledge. And like the church, leading figures naturally proclaim truths they deem indubitable. Once announced, they too are unable to take them back.

"As long as I continue to inspire people with a respectful servility toward science, they will never be able to grasp the teaching that almost led to our ruin."

•

"Very good. Thank you," said Beelzebub, his face shining. "You deserve a reward and I shall give you what is due."

"But you've forgotten about us!" shouted all the other devils in their different voices, big devils and small devils, bandy-legged devils, fat devils and thin devils, all them with fur of different color.

"What do you do?" asked Beelzebub.

"I'm the devil of technological improvement."

"I'm the devil of the division of labor."

"I'm the devil of transportation."

"I'm the devil of mass communication."

"I'm the devil of medical advancement."

"I'm the devil of higher education."

"I'm the devil of social reform."

"I'm the devil of addiction."

"I'm the devil of charity."

"I'm the devil of profits and margins."

"I'm the devil of socialism."

"I'm the devil of feminism."

They all shouted at once, pressing forward in front of Beelzebub.

"Speak briefly and one at a time," shouted Beelzebub. "You!" he said, turning to the devil of technological improvement. "What exactly do you do?"

"I get people to think that the more things they can make, and the more efficiently, the better it will be for everyone. And so people ruin their lives in order to produce more things, in spite of the fact that they are neither needed by those who have them made, nor available to those who make them."

"Good. And what about you?" Beelzebub turned to the devil of the division of labor.

"I persuade people that since things can be made more quickly and easily by machines than by people, then people must behave in the manner of machines. This brings about a deep resentment, but no one knows exactly whom to blame."

"That's excellent. And what about you?" Beelzebub turned to the devil of transportation.

"I make people think that it is important to move about as fast and far as possible from place to place. Instead of bettering their life at home, with their next door neighbors, people busy themselves going from place to place, taking great pride and pleasure in the fact that they can travel sixty-five miles an hour and faster."

Beelzebub praised him too.

The devil of mass communication came forward. He explained that his work lay in communicating to as many people as possible all the superfluous and stupid things that are done and written about in the world — just to keep everyone adequately informed.

The devil of medical advancement explained that his job was to get people to believe that the most important thing of all is to avoid pain as much as possible. Since there is no end to physical ailment, people preoccupy themselves so much with their bodies that they forget not only about the lives and needs of others, but even about their own.

The devil of higher education explained that he persuaded people that it was possible to teach children and young people how to live well, while living badly oneself and not even knowing what constitutes a good life.

The devil of social reform explained that he taught people that they can reform the depraved even though they were depraved themselves.

The devil of addiction said that he taught people to anesthetize themselves, under the influence of alcohol, pills, and all kinds of stimulants against life's troubles and suffering, instead of looking at the causes of what makes them so unhappy.

The devil of charity said that he made people inaccessible to goodness by persuading them that if they, along with everybody else, gave back a little from their abundance, then they were virtuous and did not actually have to improve their own lives.

The devil of profits and margins eagerly exclaimed that since the business of life was business he was able to suck dry people's souls.

The devil of socialism boasted that in the name of social organization and equality he excited hostility between the classes.

The devil of feminism boasted that he too, in the name of equality, excited hostility, but this hostility was between the sexes.

"I am comfort! I am fashion!" still more devils cried out and squealed as they crawled up to Beelzebub.

"Do you really think that I am so old and stupid as not to understand that if the basis of life itself is false, then everything that would otherwise damage our interests instead goes to further them?" shouted Beelzebub with a loud peal of laughter. "Enough of this! My thanks to you all."

Beelzebub opened his wings and sprang to his feet. The devils surrounded him and began to form into a chain. At one end was the devil in a cape who had invented religion; at the other end was the devil in a mantle who had invented science. These two held out their paws to one another and the circle was complete.

Then, chuckling, squealing, whistling and snorting, flicking and waving their tails, the devils began to whirl and spin around Beelzebub. Beelzebub himself danced in the middle, kicking his legs high into the air and flapping his spread wings. From above could be heard cries, wails, groans, and the gnashing of teeth.   — *The Religious Writings of Tolstoy*

ALL BROTHERS AND SISTERS

In one way or another, each of us is aware of being children of one Father. Wherever we may live and whatever language we may speak, we are all brothers and sisters and are subject to the same law of love implanted by our common Father in our hearts.

Whatever the opinions and degree of education we may have, whatever our shade of politics, whatever our philosophy of life, whatever our view of science or of economics, however ignorant or superstitious we may be, each of us knows that we all possess an equal right to life and to the good things of life. We each know that one set of people is no better nor worse than another, that we are all spiritually equal. Everyone knows this, beyond doubt; everyone feels it.

Yet at the same time we see around us the division of people into two classes — the one, laboring, oppressed, poor, and suffering, eking out an existence, the other idle, indifferent, comfortable, and wasteful. We not only see this, but voluntarily or involuntarily, in one way or another, take part in maintaining this distinction. And we cannot help suffering from the consciousness of this contradiction and our share in it. Whether we are a master or a slave, rich or poor, we cannot help constantly feeling the painful opposition between our conscience and the way things are, and the miseries resulting from it.

The toiling masses, the immense majority of humankind who are suffering under the incessant, meaningless, and hopeless toil and privation in which their whole life is swallowed up, find their worst suffering in the glaring contrast between what is and what ought to be, according to all the beliefs held by themselves and those who have brought them to that condition and keep them in it.

They know that they are oppressed and condemned to privation and darkness to serve the cravings of the minority who either keep them down or don't care. They know it, and may even say so plainly. But this knowledge increases their sufferings and constitutes its bitterest sting. The slave of antiquity knew that he or she was a slave by nature, but the laborer of today, while he feels he is a slave, knows that he ought not to be, and so he tastes the agony of Tantalus, forever desiring and never gaining what might and ought to be his.

The misery of the working classes, springing from the contradiction between what is and what ought to be, is increased tenfold by the envy and hatred engendered by their consciousness of it. And even if their toil were to become much lighter than that of the slave of ancient times, gaining an eight-hour working day and a higher wage, they are perfectly aware of the fact they make things in order to satisfy the desires of those who have the real power.

The average working person thinks to himself, "I ought to be free, equal to everyone else, and loved, but in reality I am a pawn, a slave, humiliated and hated." And he too is filled with resentment and tries to find means to escape from his position by shaking off the enemy who is overriding him. Yet he knows that one of the first conditions of Christian life is love, not in words only but in deeds. How is the "slave" to love his master?

Those who are well off live in a still more glaring inconsistency, and peculiarly enough, suffer all the more. They know that their very lives are framed on principles in direct opposition to those of Christianity, humanity, and justice. They know, deep down, that all their habits of living, which they could not give up without a great deal of discomfort, can be satisfied only through the exhausting, often fatal, toil of oppressed laborers, that is, through the most obvious and brutal violation of their stated principles. They advocate freedom and opportunity, but live so that they are dependent on the oppression of the working classes, and so that their whole lifestyle is based on the advantages gained by their oppression.

We are all brothers and sisters — and yet every morning a brother or a sister must take away *my* garbage. We are all brothers and sisters, but every day I must have a cigar, a coffee on ice, and such things, which my brothers and sisters have been wasting their health on in manufacturing, and I enjoy these things and "need" them. We are all brothers and sisters, yet I live by working in a bank, doing sales work, or a business that makes it costly for my brothers and sisters to live. We are all brothers and sisters, but I live on a salary paid me for prosecuting, judging, and condemning the thief or the prostitute whose existence the whole tenor of my life tends to bring about, and who I know ought not to be punished but reformed. We are all brothers and sisters, but I live on the salary paid to me by a government that collects taxes from those who can't afford to pay them, while those who can don't. We are all brothers and sisters, but I take a salary for preaching Christianity, which I do not myself believe in, and which only serves to hinder people from understanding what Christ really wills. We are all brothers and sisters, but I will not give the poor the benefit of my educational, medical, or literary labors except for money. We are all brothers and sisters, yet I take a salary for being ready to kill, for teaching others to kill, or for making instruments of death.

For those of us who live well, our entire lives are a constant inconsistency. The more sensitive our conscience is, the more painful this contradiction will be to us. We cannot but suffer if we live well while others barely live. Unless we turn around, the only means by which we can escape from this suffering is to blunt our conscience, but even if some of us succeed in dulling our conscience, we cannot dull our fears.

— *The Kingdom of God Is within You*

ARE WE ANY DIFFERENT?

In every era there are things we remember not only with horror, but with indignation.

We read about burnings for heresy, military colonization, whippings, and running the gauntlet, and are not only horror-struck at humankind's cruelty, but we can't imagine the mental state of those who did such things.

I knew a man, who one evening danced the evening away with a beautiful girl, but then had to retire earlier than normal in order to be awake early in the morning to make arrangements to compel a runaway soldier to be killed in running the gauntlet. After he had seen this man whipped to death, he returned to his family and ate a hearty dinner!

Terrible things like this have always occurred, things so awful we cannot understand them. We simply can't grasp the horrors of the past, how they could have been perpetrated, even if those involved did not recognize their bestial inhumanity.

But is our day so peculiar, so fortunate, that we have no such horrors, no such happenings that will be just as unbelievable and incomprehensible to our descendants? No. There are just such deeds, just such horrors, only we don't see them, as our predecessors did not see those in their day.

Yes, it is clear to us now that burning of heretics, and applying torture for eliciting truth, is not only cruel, but ridiculous. Even a child sees the absurdity of it. But the people of those times did not see it so. Sensible, educated people thought that torture was a necessity, that it was near impossible for the authorities to get along without it. The same could be said of slavery. But now it is hard to imagine the mental state of anyone who believes in slavery.

But what about the horrors of our day? What about our tortures, our slavery, our whippings? It seems to us that we no longer do such things, but this is only because we refuse to come to terms with the old, and strenuously shut our eyes to it. If we would only stop shutting our eyes to the past we would see that we are committing the same kind of horrors today, only under new forms.

If we honestly look at our past, then we would see our current situation for what it is. If we would only call bonfires, branding irons, tortures, recruiting stations by their real names, then we should find also the right name for our prison cells, jails, wars, military system, death chambers. If we would but look attentively at what was done yesterday, we would then take notice of what is going on now.

If it appears to us that it was ridiculous and cruel to cut people's heads off on the scaffold, then it would likewise be clear to us — if not even more so — that it is ridiculous and cruel to poison men, or put them into a state of solitary confinement, which is even worse than death. If it is absurd and cruel to compel peasants into being soldiers and to brand them like cattle, then it will seem equally horrific and cruel to make every man who is of proper age become a soldier.

We claim we now have no tortures, no slavery, no whippings to death, and so on. Really? Over a million men in prison, locked away in inhuman cells, whose women and children are left without enough to live on? Only the security guards, and those who build and maintain these hell-holes, seem to gain advantage from this senseless, cruel confinement.

Millions of people go to rack and ruin physically and morally in the slavery of factories around the world, which produce useless items for people who already have too much. It does not require a great deal of intelligence to see that in our day it is just the same, and our age is fecund with horrors, and that these, in the eyes of succeeding generations, will seem just as unbelievable in their cruelty and stupidity. The disease of the past continues into the present; it's just that it is not felt by those of us who profit by it.   — *Essays, Letters, Miscellanies*

THREE PARABLES

I

A weed had spread over a beautiful meadow. And in order to get rid of it the tenants of the meadow mowed it, but the weed only increased in consequence. Then the kind, wise master came to visit the tenants of the meadow, and among the other good advice which he gave them, he told them that they shouldn't mow the weed, since that only made it grow the more, but instead they should pull it up by the roots.

But either because the tenants of the meadow did not, among the other prescriptions of the good master, take heed of his advice not to mow down the weed, but to pull it up, or because they did not understand him, or because, according to their calculations, it seemed foolish to do such laborious work, the result was that his advice not to mow the weed but to pull it up was not followed, just as if he had never proffered it, and the tenants went on mowing the weed and spreading it.

And although, during the succeeding years, there were people that reminded the tenants of the meadow of the advice of the kind, wise master, they did not heed them and continued to do as before, so that mowing of the weed as soon as it began to spring up became not only a custom but even a sacred tradition, and the meadow grew more and more infested. And the matter went so far that the meadow grew nothing but weeds, and the people lamented this and invented all kinds of means to correct the evil. But the only one they did not use was that which had long ago been prescribed by their kind, wise master.

As time went on it occurred to one man who saw the wretched condition into which the meadow had fallen, and who found among the master's forgotten prescriptions the rule not to mow the weed, but to pull it up by the root — it occurred to the man, I say, to remind the tenants of the meadow that they were acting foolishly, and that their folly had long ago been pointed out by the kind, wise master.

But what do you think! Instead of putting credence in the correctness of this man's recollections, they took exception to them and began to abuse him. Some called him a conceited fool who imagined that he was the only one to understand the master's regulations; others called him a malicious false interpreter and slanderer; still others, forgetting that he was not giving them his own opinions, but was only reminding them of the prescriptions of the wise master whom they all revered, called him a dangerous man because he wished to pull up the weed and deprive them of their meadow. "He says we ought not to mow the meadow," said they, purposely suppressing the fact that the man did not say that but only that they should pull the weeds up by the roots instead of mowing it, "but if we do not destroy the weed, then it will spread and wholly ruin our meadow. And why was the meadow granted to us if we must train the weed in it?"

And the general impression that this man was either a fool or a false interpreter, or had the purpose of injuring the people, became so taken for granted that everyone reproached and ridiculed him. And no matter how earnestly he denied the claim that he did not desire to spread the weed, but on the contrary considered the destruction of the weed as one of the chief duties of the agriculturist, just as it was meant by the good, wise master whose words he merely repeated, still they would not listen to him because they had made up their minds that he was either a conceited fool misinterpreting the good, wise master's words, or a villain trying to induce them not to destroy the weeds but to protect and spread them more widely.

This kind of thing has taken place in my own case in my attempts to point out to people Christ's teaching about the nonresistance of evil by violence. Either because people do not notice this command, or because they do not understand it, or because its fulfillment seems too difficult, as time has passed by, the more this command has been forgotten, and, consequently, the farther the manner of our lives have departed from this command. And now this command seems to people something new, strange, unheard-of, and even foolish. And I, like the man who reminded the people of the good, wise master's prescription to refrain from mowing the weed, but to pull it up by the roots, am one who is misunderstood and maligned.

In reply to my reminder that according to Christ's teaching in order to annihilate evil we must not employ violence against it, but must destroy it from the root with love, people say: "We will not listen to him, he is a fool; he advises us not to oppose evil and so evil will overwhelm us."

But I've only pointed out what Christ taught, that evil cannot be eradicated by evil; that all resistance to evil by violence only leads to more evil; that according to Christ's teaching evil is eradicated by good. "Bless them that curse you, pray for them that abuse you, do good to them that hate you, love your enemies, and you will have no enemies."

I have tried to remind the people that, according to Christ's teaching, our whole life is a battle against evil, but this battle must be fought by reason and love. One cannot fight evil with evil, or evil on its own terms.

People falsely accuse me of saying that we must not resist evil. And everyone whose lives are based on violence, and to whom in consequence violence is dear, are now quick to misconstrue my words, and at the same time Christ's words. To them, the way of nonresistance is incredible, stupid, godless, and dangerous. And so the majority calmly continue under the guise of destroying evil to spread it more widely.

II

There were some people dealing in flour, butter, milk, and all kinds of foodstuffs. And as each one wanted to receive the greatest profit and to become rich as soon as possible, all these people got more and more into the habit of adulterating their goods with cheap and injurious mixtures. With the flour they mixed bran and lime, they put oleo into their butter, they put water and even chalk into their milk. And until these goods reached the consumers all went well: the wholesale traders sold them to the retailers, and the retailers distributed them in small quantities.

There were many stores and shops, and the wares, it seemed, sold very rapidly. And the retailers were satisfied. But the city consumers, those that did not raise their own produce and were therefore obliged to buy it, found it very harmful and disagreeable. The flour was bad, the butter and milk were bad, but as there were no other goods except those adulterated to be had in the city markets, the city consumers continued to buy them, and they complained because the food tasted bad and was unwholesome. They blamed themselves and ascribed it to the wretched way in which the food was prepared. Meantime the tradesmen continued more and more flagrantly to adulterate their foodstuffs with cheap foreign ingredients. Thus passed a sufficiently long time. The city people were all displeased, but no one had the resolution to express his dissatisfaction.

It happened that a housekeeper who had always given her family food and drink of her own make came to the city. This woman had spent her whole life in the preparation of food, and though she was not a famous cook, still she knew very well how to bake nutritious bread and to cook good dinners.

This woman bought various items in the city and began to bake and cook. Her loaves did not rise, her cakes were tasteless. She set her milk, but there was no cream. The housekeeper instantly came to the conclusion that her purchases were poor.

She examined them, and her suspicions were confirmed. She found lime in the flour, oleo in the butter, even chalk in the milk. Having found that all the materials she had bought were adulterated, the housekeeper went to the markets and began to accuse the tradesmen and to demand that they should either stock their shops with good, nutritious, unadulterated articles, or else cease to trade and close up shop.

But the tradesmen paid no attention and told the housekeeper that their goods were first rate, that the whole city had been buying them for many years, and that they even had medals, and they showed her their medals on their signs. But the housekeeper did not give in.

"I don't need any medals," she said, "but wholesome food, so that my children and I may not have stomach troubles from it."

"Apparently, my good woman, you have never seen genuine flour and butter," the tradesmen said, showing her the white, pure-looking flour in varnished bins, the wretched imitation of butter lying in neat dishes, and the white fluid in glittering transparent jars.

"Of course I know them," replied the housekeeper, "because I've spent my whole life dealing with them, and I have cooked with them and have eaten them. Your goods are adulterated. Here is the proof of it," she said, displaying the spoiled bread, the oleo in the cakes, and the sediment in the milk. "You ought to throw all this stuff into the dump or burn it, and then sell unadulterated goods instead."

And the woman kept standing in front of the shops, incessantly crying out her one message to the purchasers who came by, and the purchasers began to be troubled.

Then perceiving that this audacious housekeeper was likely to hurt their business, the tradesmen said to the purchasers:

"Look here, gentlemen, this woman is a lunatic! She wants people to perish of starvation. She insists on our burning up and destroying all our provisions. What would you have to eat if we should heed her and refuse to sell you our goods? Do not listen to her, she is a coarse countrywoman, and she is no judge of provisions, and it is nothing but envy that makes her attack us. She is poor and wants everyone else to be as poor as she is."

Thus spoke the tradesmen to the gathering throng, purposely hiding the fact that the woman wanted, not that all provisions should be destroyed, but that good ones should be substituted for bad.

And thereupon the throng began to insult the woman. Yet she assured them that she had no wish to destroy the food-stuffs, that, on the contrary, her whole life had been devoted to feeding others, but that she only wanted that those who took upon themselves the feeding of the people should not poison them with deleterious adulterations pretending to be edible. Though she pleaded her cause eloquently, they refused to hear her because their minds were made up, asserting that she wanted to deprive people of the food which they needed.

III

Some travelers were making a journey. They happened to lose their way, so that they found themselves proceeding, not on a smooth road, but across a bog, among clumps of bushes, briers, and fallen trees, which blocked their progress. Even to move grew more and more difficult.

Then the travelers divided into two parties. One group decided not to stop, but to keep going in the direction that they had been going, assuring themselves and the others that they had not wandered from the right road and were sure to reach their journey's end.

The other party decided that, as the direction in which they were now going was evidently not the right one — otherwise they would long ago have reached the journey's end — it was necessary to find the right road, and in order to find it, it was necessary that without delay they should move as rapidly as possible in all directions. All the travelers were divided between these two opinions: some decided to keep going straight ahead; the others decided to venture out in all directions. But there was one man who, without sharing either opinion, suggested that before continuing in the direction in which they had been going, or beginning to spread out in all directions, hoping that by this means they might find the right way, they should first of all pause and deliberate on their situation, and then after due deliberation decide on one thing or the other.

But the travelers were so worked up, were so alarmed at their situation, were so keen to flatter themselves with the hope that they had not lost their way but had only temporarily wandered from the road and would soon find it again, and, above all, they had such a desire to forget their terror by moving about, that this opinion was met with universal indignation, with reproaches, and with the ridicule of those of both parties.

"It is the advice of weakness, cowardice, sloth," they said.

"What a fine way to reach the end of our journey, sitting down and not moving from the place!" cried others.

"It for this that we are men, and this is why we are given strength, to struggle and labor, conquering obstacles, and not pusillanimously giving in to them," exclaimed still others.

And, in spite of what the man said, "how if we proceeded in a wrong direction without changing it, we should never attain our goal, but go farther from it, and how we should never attain it either if we kept flying from one direction to another, and how the only means of attaining our goal was by taking observation from the sun or the stars and thus finding what direction we must take to reach it, and having chosen it to stick to it — and how to do this it was necessary first of all to halt, and to halt not for the purpose of stopping, but to find the right way and then unfalteringly to go on it, and how for either case it was necessary to stop and consider" — in spite of his words of caution, they refused to heed him.

So the first group of travelers went off in the direction in which they had been going, and the second group kept changing their course. But neither group succeeded in attaining their journey's end; and even today they have not yet escaped from the bushes and the briers, but are still lost.

Exactly the same thing has happened to me. I have attempted to express my doubts as to whether the road which we have taken through the dark forest of the labor question and through the all-swallowing bog of the endless armament of the nations is really the right route by which we ought to go, that it is very possible that we have lost our way, and that, therefore, it might be good to stop moving, and first of all consider by means of the universal and eternal laws of truth revealed to us what the direction is which we intend to go.

We have lost our way and are suffering in consequence. It would seem that the first thing we should do is to direct our energies, not to the confirmation of the movement that has seduced us into the false position where we are, but to the cessation of it. It would seem clear that as soon as we stopped we might in measure grasp our situation and discover the direction in which we ought to go in order to attain true happiness, not for one person, not for one class of people, but for all the people.

But how is it? People come up with every possible suggestion, but fail to hit upon the one thing that might bring them salvation, or at least ameliorate their condition. I mean that we should pause for a moment and not go on increasing our misfortunes by all our fallacious activity. People all over the world are conscious of the wretchedness of their lives and are doing all they can to correct it, but the one thing that would assuredly help them most they are unwilling to do, and the advice given them to do it, more than anything else, rouses their indignation.

If there were any possibility of doubting the fact that we have gone astray, then this treatment of the advice to "think it over"

proves more distinctly than anything else how hopelessly astray
we have gone and how great is our despair.

— Essays, Letters, Miscellanies

UNIVERSAL HYPOCRISY

People talk of the time when everybody will be well fed and
clothed, when everybody will be united from one end of the
world to the other by telephones and flying machines, when
all the working classes will be properly educated and everyone will be able to read newspapers and learn all the sciences.
But so what? Why is this important if we do not speak and
act in accordance with the truth? How can we be united in the
truth or even approximate it, if we do not even live the truth we
know, or pretend to regard as truth what we know to be false?

No improvement in life is possible so long as we are hypo-
critical and hide the truth from ourselves. So long as we do not
recognize that our union, and therefore our welfare, is only possible in the truth, and do not put the recognition and profession
of the truth revealed to us higher than everything else, nothing
can move forward.

All the material improvements may be realized, but this alone
will not improve the condition of humanity. But only let each
person, according to his powers, live out the truth he knows,
or at least cease to support the falsehoods in the place of the
truth, and at once, in this year, we should see such change as
we do not dare to hope for within a century — the liberation of
all and the reign of truth upon earth.

Not without good reason did Christ speak most harshly
against hypocrites and hypocrisy. It is not theft nor robbery
nor murder nor fornication, but falsehood, the special falsehood of hypocrisy, which corrupts people, brutalizes them and
makes them vindictive, destroys all distinction between right
and wrong, deprives them of what is the true meaning of all

real human life, and debars them from all progress toward perfection.

Those who do something wrong on account of ignorance provoke sympathy with their victims and repugnance for their actions; they do harm only to those they attack. But those who know the truth and do evil masked by hypocrisy injure themselves and their victims, and thousands of others as well, who are led astray by the falsehood with which the wrongdoing is disguised.

Thieves, robbers, murderers, and cheats, those who commit crimes recognized by themselves and everyone else as evil, serve as an example of what ought not to be done, and deter others from similar crimes. But those who commit the same thefts, robberies, murders, and other crimes, disguising them under all kinds of religious or scientific or humanitarian justifications, as landowners, merchants, manufacturers, and government officials do, provoke others to imitation, and so do harm not only to those who are directly the victims of their crimes, but to thousands and millions of men whom they corrupt by obliterating their sense of the distinction between right and wrong.

A single fortune gained by trading in goods necessary to the people or in goods pernicious in their effects, or by financial speculations, or by acquiring land at a low price the value of which is increased by the needs of the population, or by an industry ruinous to the health and life of those employed in it, or by military or civil service of the state, or by any employment which trades on men's evil instincts — a single fortune acquired in any of these ways, not only with the sanction, but even with the approval of the leaders in society, and masked with an ostentation of philanthropy, corrupts people incomparably more than millions of thefts and robberies committed against the recognized forms of law and punishable as crimes.

A single execution carried out by prosperous, educated people uninfluenced by passion, with the approval and assistance of Christian ministers, and represented as something necessary and even just, is infinitely more corrupting and brutalizing to people than thousands of murders committed by uneducated working people under the influence of passion.

Every war, even the most humanely conducted, with all its ordinary consequences, the destruction of harvests, robberies, the license and debauchery, and the murder with the justifications of its necessity and justice, the exaltation and glorification of military exploits, the worship of the flag, the patriotic sentiments, the feigned solicitude for the wounded, and so on, does more in one year to pervert our minds than thousands of robberies, murders, and arsons perpetrated during hundreds of years by individuals under the influence of passion.

The luxurious expenditure of a single respectable and so-called honorable family, even within the conventional limits, consuming as it does the produce of as many days of labor as would suffice to provide for thousands living in privation, does more to pervert our minds than thousands of the violent orgies of coarse laborers, officers, and workmen of drunken and debauched habits, who smash up glasses and crockery for amusement.

One solemn religious procession, one service, one sermon from the altar-steps or the pulpit, in which the preacher does not believe, produces incomparably more evil than thousands of swindling tricks, adulteration of food, and so on.

We talk of the hypocrisy of the Pharisees, but the hypocrisy of our society far surpasses that of the Pharisees. When we who profit by a system based on violence, and at the same time claim to love our neighbor but fail to pay attention to what we are doing in our daily life to our neighbor, when we fail to see the contradiction of our own modern lives, we are like a brigand who has spent his life in robbing people, and who, caught at last, knife in hand, in the very act of striking his shrieking victim, should declare that he had no idea that what he was doing was disagreeable to the man he had robbed and was prepared to murder. Just as this robber and murderer could not deny what was evident to everyone, so those living upon the privations of the oppressed classes cannot honestly persuade themselves and others that they desire the welfare of those they plunder, and that they do not know how the advantages they enjoy are obtained.

How can we honestly claim we do not know about the hundreds of thousands of people in our prisons who are there on account of us trying to guarantee the security of our property and tranquility? How can we say that we do not know about the law courts in which we take part, and which, at our initiative, condemn those who have attacked our property or our security to prison, exile, or forced labor, whereby human beings no worse than those who condemn them are ruined and corrupted? We cannot pretend that we do not see the armed policeman who marches up and down beneath our windows to guarantee our security while we eat our delicious dinner, or look at the new piece at the theater, or that we are unaware of the existence of the soldiers who will make their appearance with guns and cartridges directly if our property or nation is attacked.

We know very well that we are only allowed to go on eating our dinner, to finish seeing the new play, or to enjoy to the end the ball, the Christmas fête, the promenade, the races or the hunt, thanks to the policeman's revolver and the soldier's rifle, which will shoot down the famished outcast who has been robbed of his share and who looks round the corner with covetous eyes at our pleasures, ready to interrupt them instantly, were not the policeman and the soldier there prepared to run up at our first call for help.

And therefore just as a brigand caught in broad daylight in the act cannot persuade us that he did not lift his knife in order to rob his victim of his purse, and had no thought of killing him, we too, cannot honestly persuade ourselves or others that the soldiers and policemen around us are not to guard us, but only for defense against foreign foes, and to regulate traffic and fêtes and reviews. We cannot persuade ourselves and others that we do not know that people do not like dying of hunger, bereft of the right to gain their subsistence from the earth on which they live; that they do not like working underground, in the water, or in stifling heat, for ten to fourteen hours a day, at night in airless factories to manufacture objects for our pleasure. One would imagine it impossible to deny what is so obvious. Yet it is denied.

— *The Kingdom of God Is within You*

DIFFICULT, BUT DOABLE

Why don't we just do what Jesus told us to do? Why do so many of us admire Christ's teaching, but fail to carry it out?

From every corner I hear one and the same reply: Christ's teachings are good, but too difficult; they are too hard to obey. His words are laudable, and life according to his words would be far better than what we are living now, but we cannot live out this better way because it is too difficult.

If one understands "difficult" to mean that it is hard to sacrifice the momentary satisfaction of desire for the sake of a great good, then why do we not say that it is too difficult to plow in order to obtain grain for bread or to plant apple trees in order to get apples? That it is necessary to overcome difficulties to gain a great advantage is known to anyone endowed with the rudiments of reason. And yet we say that Christ's teaching is admirable, but is impractical because it is difficult. Difficult, because to follow it we must deny ourselves something we had possessed until then. It is as if we had never heard that it is sometimes better to endure and forgo than to suffer nothing and always satisfy our lusts.

We are more than our desires, and Christ's teaching shows us how to be free from their dictates. Will we pay heed, despite the difficulty?

In the dark I hurt my hand and my knee seeking the door. Someone enters with a light, and I see the door. When I see the door I no longer have to knock myself against the wall. Still less is it reasonably possible to assert that though I see the door and consider it better to pass through the door, it is difficult to do so and I therefore wish to continue to knock my knee against the wall....

There is an obvious misunderstanding in the thought that Christ's teaching is good but that we are too weak and wicked to follow it. But it is evidently not a mere error in thought, but something else that bogs us down.

Good Christians say that Christ's teaching is an ideal, but not something we can fulfill here and now, in this life. Our consolation lies elsewhere, in the future and in the blissful state of eternal life. Philosophers, sociologists, and common thought concur, but from a different standpoint. Historical and social progress is slow, they say, and we have yet to endure the sociological processes of human development. Yet life itself is improving and will eventually perfect itself, but not now.

People come to a farm and there find everything necessary for life: a house with all the necessary utensils, barns full of grain, cellars, vaults containing all kinds of supplies. In the yard are agricultural implements, tools, horses, cows, sheep, and a complete inventory — all that is necessary for a well-supplied life. People from around the area come to this farm and begin to make use of all they find there, but each only for himself, not thinking of leaving anything either for those who are there in the house or for those who will come later. Each wishes to have everything for himself. Each hastens to make use of what he can seize, and the destruction of everything begins — strife and a struggle for possession. A milk cow, unshorn sheep, and sheep bearing young are killed for meat; fires are fed with benches and carts and people fight for milk and grain, and spill, scatter, destroy more than they use. No one eats a morsel quietly; he eats and snarls. Someone who is stronger comes and takes the morsel away, and another takes it from him. Having tormented themselves, these people, beaten and hungry, leave the place.

Again the farm owner rearranges the place so that people could live in it. And again the same thing occurs, and again, and again, and again. Then a teacher comes along who says to the others, "Brothers, we are not acting rightly. See how many goods there are in the place and how well it is all arranged! There is enough for us all and there will be a surplus for those who come after us; only let us live reasonably. Let us stop taking from one another, but instead start helping one another. Let us sow, and plow, and tend the cattle, and we will all be able to live well."

And it happened that some people understood what the teacher said, and those who understood began to do as he instructed them; they ceased fighting and taking from one another and began to work. But the rest, who had either not heard the words of the teacher or had heard but did not believe him, did not follow his advice, but fought as before and spoiled their host's goods and went away. Others came and the same thing happened. Those who heeded the teacher kept on saying the same thing: "Do not fight, do not destroy the host's goods, and it will be better for you all. Do as the teacher says."

But there were still many who had not heard or did not believe, and matters continued to go on in the old way. At last a time came when everyone knew about the teacher's words, and everyone understood them, and not only understood them but acknowledged that it was God himself who spoke through the teacher and that the teacher was himself God, and all believed in every word the teacher spoke. And it is told that after this, instead of living as the teacher advised, the brawls continued, worse than before, and the people started thrashing one another, and all began to say that this is how things are and that nothing else is possible.

What does it all mean? Even cattle manage to eat their fodder so that it should not be wasted uselessly, but we, having learned

how we might live better and believing that God himself commanded us to do so, live even worse, because we claim that it is
impossible to live otherwise.

What could the people on the farm have imagined, which
let them, having believed the teacher's words, continue to live
as before, stealing from one another, fighting, and ruining the
goods and themselves? The teacher had told them: "Your life
on this farm is bad; live better and your life will become good."
But they imagined that the teacher had condemned any kind of
life on the farm, and had promised them another, a good life,
not at that farm but somewhere else. And so they decided that
this farm was a temporary inn, and that it was not worthwhile
arranging to live well in it, but that it was only necessary to be
on the alert not to miss the good life promised in another place.

We have heard everything and understood it all. But we have
let slip past our ears what the teacher actually said. We have
forgotten that we must create our own happiness here, on this
farm at which we have met. We have imagined that our earthly
life was an inn and that the real, our real home is somewhere
else. And from this has come our amazing argument that the
words of the teacher are very admirable, and even the words of
God himself, but that it is now too difficult to obey them.

And now we destroy ourselves and expect that someone will
come and help us — Christ on the clouds with the sound of
trumpets, or a historic law, or a law of the differentiation and
integration of forces. But no one will help us unless we begin to
act right where we are. It is not help from heaven we need. We
simply need to stop destroying ourselves.   — *What I Believe*

THE PRICE OF PROGRESS

There is no doubt that never in history has such material progress been made in mastering the powers of Nature as during our
century. At the same time, there is no doubt that never before

has there been such rampant immorality. The material progress achieved in this century has truly been great; but that progress has been bought, and is being bought, by a neglect of the most elementary demands of duty as humanity has never before been guilty of.

Railroads, printing presses, tunnels, phonographs, X-rays, and so forth, are very good. They are all very good, but what is also good — good, as Ruskin says, beyond comparison with anything else — are human lives, such as those of which millions are now mercilessly ruined for the acquisition of railways and tunnels, which instead of beautifying life disfigure it.

To this the usual reply is that technologies are already being invented, and will continue to be invented, precisely to put an end to all the various miseries that plague human life. But this is simply not true. As long as we do not consider one another as brothers and sisters and do not consider human lives the most sacred of all things — on no account to be sacrificed — that is, as long as we do not treat each other as beings created by God, we will always find ways to ruin one another's lives.

A time may come that those who destroy human lives for their own profit will be shamed by public opinion or otherwise will be compelled by law to provide safer measures. But as long as we don't live before God, we will, even after providing safer measures, find other means to exploit human lives for the sake of profit.

It is easy to conquer Nature, to build railways, ocean liners, and so forth, if we are not too concerned about sparing human lives. The Egyptian pharaohs were proud of their pyramids, and we find them amazing, while forgetting the thousands upon thousands of slaves whose lives were sacrificed for their erection. And in the same way, we are impressed by so many of today's technological advances, but forget what we pay for these things. How can we feel proud of all this?

Under the surface of material betterment always lies a vast sea of suffering. What we call "progress" is none other than the ongoing quest to fill the emptiness of our selfish lives. It is the result of our demand for an insane and rich life of comfort, obtained by enslaving people — people who are cold and hungry and bound by want — in a system that benefits the few. If history teaches us anything, it teaches us this.

All of us know that railways and factories are not for the betterment of the people. We know perfectly well that the engineers and capitalists behind them are not thinking about the common good or about the average working person, but about how to make a profit and how to make the best possible use of them. An engineer builds a railway for the government. Why? To facilitate wars. Or he builds one for a capitalist. Why? For financial advancement.

We now know how to investigate protoplasm and analyze the stars, but do we really know what kind of flour is best to use or how to make an affordable, efficient stove to bake our bread? We have invented marvelous means of communication, but what have these improvements really done for us? We have cataloged two million insects, but have we domesticated a single animal since biblical times, when all our animals had long been domesticated? The elk and the deer and the partridge and the grouse and the wood-hen are still wild. From the ancient Egyptians and Hebrews, when wheat and lentils were already cultivated, down to the present time, not a single plant has been added for the nourishment of the people except potatoes, and these were not discovered by science. Are we any further along?
— *What Is to Be Done?*

WHO *IS* RESPONSIBLE?

In a wicker basket all the ends are so hidden away that it is difficult to find them. Similarly, in our current political and social system the responsibility for the crimes committed is so hidden away that people will commit the most atrocious acts without seeing their responsibility for them.

In ancient times tyrants got credit for the crimes they committed, but in our day the most atrocious infamies, inconceivable under the Neros, are perpetrated and no one gets blamed for them.

How is this possible? One set of people have suggested, another set have proposed, a third have reported, a fourth have decided, a fifth have confirmed, a sixth have given the order, and a seventh set have carried it out. They gas, they beat to death women, old men, and innocent people, they shoot and torture people by hundreds and thousands, or massacre millions in war, or break people's hearts in solitary confinement, and ruin their souls in the corruption of war, and no one is responsible.

At the bottom of the social scale soldiers, armed with weapons of every kind, murder people, and are absolutely convinced that the responsibility for their actions rests solely on the officers who command them.

At the top of the scale — the presidents, congressmen, and parliaments decree these tortures and murders and military conscription and are fully convinced that since they are either placed in authority by God or by the society they govern, which demands such decrees from them, they cannot be held responsible.

Between these two are all those who oversee the murders and other acts of violence. They too are fully convinced that the responsibility is not on their shoulders but on their superiors who give the orders. How are they to blame if they, who are at the bottom of the scale, are expected to carry out such orders?

The authority who gives the orders and the authority who executes them at the two extreme ends meet together like the two ends of a ring; they support and rest on one another and enclose all that lies within the ring.

Without the conviction that there is a person or persons who will take the responsibility of one's acts, not one soldier, for example, would ever lift a hand to kill. Without the conviction that it is the will of the people, not a single king, emperor, president, or parliament would order murders or acts of violence. And without the conviction that there are persons of a higher grade who will take the responsibility, and people of a lower grade who require such acts for their welfare, not one of the intermediate class would superintend such deeds.

Our society is so organized that wherever a person is placed in the social scale, his irresponsibility is the same. We have conveniently created a world in which we are bound together by the act of throwing the responsibility of our actions on to one another. No one is to blame, and death prevails.

— The Kingdom of God Is within You

FROM THE HEIGHT OF OUR "GREATNESS"

I happened once to visit a friend. Passing through the first room, I noticed two females. This was odd, since my friend was a bachelor. A skinny, yellow, older-looking woman, who was only thirty, with a scarf thrown over her shoulder, was briskly doing something over the table with her hands, jerking nervously, as if in a fit. Opposite to her sat a little girl, who was also doing something, jerking in the same way. They both seemed to be suffering from some kind of nervous disorder. I came nearer and looked closer at what they were doing.

They glanced up at me and then continued their work as attentively as before.

In front of them were spread tobacco and cigarettes. They were making cigarettes. The woman rubbed the tobacco fine between the palms of her hands, caught it up by a machine, put on the tubes, and threw them to the girl. The girl folded the papers, put them over the cigarette, threw it aside, and took up another.

All this was performed with such speed, with such dexterity, that it was impossible to describe it. I expressed how amazed I was at their speed. "I have been at this business fourteen years," said the woman.

"Is it hard work?"

"Yes. My chest aches, and the air is thick with tobacco."

But it was not necessary for her to have said so: one only had to look at her or at the girl. Seeing her at this work one would have thought that she had a strong constitution, but she was already fast becoming debilitated.

My friend, a kindhearted man of liberal views, hired these women to make him and his colleagues cigarettes. He pays them for it. He has the money: what harm is there in it?

But my friend gets up at noon. His evenings, from six to two, he spends at cards or at the piano. He eats and drinks, while other people do the work for him. And he now has acquired for himself a new pleasure — smoking.

Here are a woman and a girl, who scarcely earn their living by transforming themselves into little machines, and pass their days ruining their lives by breathing tobacco. My friend has money, but not money he has really worked for. He prefers playing cards to making cigarettes for himself. He gives these poor souls money, but only just enough to make cigarettes for him, not enough for them to live a decent life.

When I think of myself, I like to be clean and like the way clean clothes feel. I therefore pay someone to clean my clothes, on condition, of course, that my shirts, which I change twice a day, are clean. Do I care that my clean shirts tax the washerwoman's entire strength? Do I really care that she is now dead?

What is wrong in this?

Others will continue to buy and hire, whether I do so or not. They will take advantage of people's plight, forcing them to make velvets and dainties, and they will buy them up whether I do or not. So they will also hire people to make cigarettes and to wash shirts. Why should I, then, deprive myself of velvets, sweets, cigarettes, and clean shirts, when they will be produced and sold anyway? What's the point of wearing a dirty shirt or in making my own cigarettes? How will this help anyone? What difference would it make?

So ask thousands who try to justify the way they live. Had we all not wandered so far from truth, we wouldn't have to answer this question. What difference would it make? What difference would it make to wear my shirt for a week, instead of for a day, to make my own cigarettes or stop smoking altogether?

The obvious difference would be this: I would have more to give those who, exhausted, are barely able, if at all, to make ends meet.

The skeptic will reply, "One drop won't help to swell the sea. The poor will always be exploited."

What would you or I do if we came among some savages who offered us some delicious chops to eat, but before imbibing we learned that these juicy chops were made of a human prisoner who had been slain in order to make them? We would think it disgusting to eat human flesh, no matter how delicious the cutlets may be, and would refuse to eat. Even if the loss of life had already occurred, we would refuse.

But this is what we are doing by living as we are. We methodically create conditions where bread and labor are stolen from work-worn masses. We live lavishly, as if there were no connection whatever between the dying washerwoman, the child-prostitute, women worn out by making cigarettes, or whatever, and by all the exhausting labor in the world that feeds our fat stomachs. We do not want to see the fact that if we stopped living such overindulgent, comfortable lives, there would not be so many people whose labor exhausts their strength to live.

It appears to us that their sufferings are one thing, and our lives another, and that we, living as we do, are only living the way everyone else would, including the poor, if they had the chance. And yet when we read our history books about how the Romans lived, we gasp at the inhumanity of the heartless aristocracy, who gorged themselves with fine dishes and delicious wines while people went starving. We shake our heads and wonder at the barbarism of our forefathers, who provided themselves with orchestras and theaters while enslaving whole peoples to keep up their plantations and gardens. From the height of our greatness, we are dumbfounded at their inhumanity. Why aren't we dumbfounded by our own?

In Matthew's Gospel it says that we are to "produce fruit in keeping with repentance," that the ax is already at the root of the trees, "and every tree that does not produce good fruit will be cut down and thrown into the fire" (Matt. 3:8–10). Yet we are so self-assured that the good tree bearing good fruit is we ourselves, and that these words apply to others, not to us. We gloss over these words and feel quite assured that this terrible thing has not happened to us, but to some other people. But it is for this very reason we do not see that this has happened to us and is taking place in our midst. We do not hear, we do not see, and we do not understand with our heart.

— *What Is to Be Done?*

THE INEXHAUSTIBLE RUBLE

In today's economy we have lost all common sense. It's as if some ants were to take the products of labor out of the foundations and carry them to the top of the hill, making the foundation narrower and narrower, thus enlarging the top, and by that means making their fellows pass also from the foundation to the top.

Instead of a life of honest labor, we have created the ideal of a purse with an "inexhaustible ruble." The well-off arrange this ruble for themselves by various means. And in order to enjoy it, they locate themselves in neighborhoods and towns where nothing is produced, but everything is swallowed up.

The working people, swindled in order that we may have this magic ruble, try to follow us, chasing after the fairy ruble, which tempts them. A few manage to lift themselves up, but the majority only make their plight worse, finding themselves more slavishly dependent than ever.

If I truly want to help others in need, then it is clear that I must first cease to plunder and tempt them. But I, by means of the most complicated cunning, have made myself owner of this said ruble. In other words, I compel hundreds and thousand of people, by my very lifestyle, to work for me and for my wants. All the while, I imagine I pity them and want to help them. It is as if I were sitting on someone's neck, and, having crushed that person, I compel him to carry me, while still riding on his shoulders. I then convince myself, and others, that I feel sorry for him, and would do most anything to ease his condition; that is, anything but get off his back.

If I genuinely want to help the poor, then I need to cease living in a way that keeps them poor. I may want to better people's lot in life, yet I get up in the morning at my leisure, and then enjoy a lifestyle that depends on the services of hundreds who barely eke out an existence. And I come to help them! — these who rise at five, or who work at midnight, sleep but little and feed on less, but who know how to plow, to reap, to put a handle on an ax, to mend fences, to sew. These are people who by their own strength and perseverance and self-restraint are a hundred times stronger, if not physically then in character, than I who come to help them.

These people put me to shame. Even those who live on the streets, whom we call "good-for-nothings," are a hundred times more industrious than I — that is, what they take from others and what they give to them is a thousand times more to their credit than mine when I count what I receive from others and what I give to them in return. And to such people I go and try to help?

I want to help the poor. But of the two, who is the poorer? No one is poorer than I am. I am the weak, good-for-nothing parasite, who can exist only in very protected conditions, who can live only when thousands of people sweat to support this life of mine, which is not useful to anyone. And I, this very caterpillar that eats up the leaves of a tree, want to help the growth and the health of the tree and to cure it.

Look at my life. I eat, talk, listen; then I eat, write or read, which are only talking and listening in another form. I eat again and play. Then eat, talk, and listen, and finally eat and go to sleep. This is my entire life. And in order that I may enjoy this life, it is necessary for thousands of others to work with their hands: those who drive me hither and yon, those who cook and wait on me, those who keep my house warm and clean, and so on. And all these men and women work hard all day (and often nights) and every day, just so I can eat, talk, play, and sleep.

And I imagine that I am able to help others!

— What Is to Be Done?

MODERN SLAVERY

For the most part, slavery has been officially abolished. But in reality, it has not.

Slavery allows some people to live off the labor of others without having to actually labor for themselves. Slavery exists wherever one person, while not working himself, makes — whether forcibly or by necessity — another person work without enabling the one who works to enjoy the same benefits as he. Thus, wherever there are people, as in the case with all the developed countries, who by means of coercion (i.e., state-authorized force) utilize the labor of others, and consider such to be their right, and others who submit to this violence, considering it to be either their lot or duty — there is slavery in its most dreadful proportions.

Slavery exists because those who are strong can overpower those who are weak. Slavery today exists in three basic modes of operation: personal and military violence, land-taxes (maintained by military force), and direct and indirect taxes placed on all the people. We do not see this as slavery because each of these forms has received new justification.

Personal violence, for example, is justified in the name of self-defense or on the moral grounds of defending one's country against its perceived enemies. It still amounts to the same thing as of old: the conquered submitting to the victor. Land is also confiscated as before, but now it is justified as a recompense for services rendered to an imaginary common good. In reality this is the same as forcibly depriving people of resources and enslaving them. Finally, the monetary violence committed today, by means of taxation, is supposedly done for the sake of the common liberty and welfare of all. But in fact it is the same slavery as before, only an impersonal one.

Whether violence finds its expression in princes with their courtiers who come, kill, and burn down villages, or in the fact that slave owners take labor or money for the land from their slaves, and enforce payment by means of armed force, or by putting taxes on others, and riding armed to and fro in the villages, or in the circumstances of a home department collecting money through government agents and police, in one word, as long as all this is maintained by means of force, even if under the law, there is no honest distribution of wealth. There is slavery.

If a pail leaks, there must be a hole. On looking at the bottom of the pail, however, we may imagine that the water is running through different imaginary cracks on the outside. But no matter how many cracks we try to fill, the pail will not cease from leaking. In order to put a stop to the leakage, we must find the place out of which the water runs, and stop it from leaking from the inside.

The same holds true with the problem of the unjust and unequal distribution of wealth, where working people don't have enough to live on and all the wealth trickles away from the people.

Are we then to make capital and the land social property? If this means the use of force, then, no. This would only be stopping from the outside those holes from which we imagine water trickles away. In order to prevent wealth going from the hands of working people to the nonworking, it is necessary to discover from inside the hole through which the leakage takes place.

Wherein lies the hole? What keeps it open? It is the violence of the armed over the unarmed, by means of which people are carried away from their labor, and the land, and the productions of labor are taken away from the people. For as long as there exist institutions of violence that grant the right for some to exercise violence, there will be those who have what they haven't worked for and those who lack what they deserve. In short, there will be slavery.   — *What Is to Be Done?*

4

The Life of Faith

THOUGHTS ON GOD

I

God is for me what I strive for, and thus what constitutes my life. Therefore for me God *is;* but God is necessarily such that I cannot comprehend or name him.

If I understood God, I would have reached him, and there would be nothing to strive after; there would be no life. And yet, though I cannot understand or name him, I know him and the direction that points me toward him. Of this I am most certain.

I do not comprehend him, yet I am always anxious when I am without him, and only when I am with him am I at peace. What is stranger still is that to know him more and better I must draw nearer to him, and I wish to do so — in that is my life; but such drawing nearer in no way increases, and cannot increase, my knowledge. On the contrary, every endeavor of the imagination to know God more definitely (for instance, as my Creator, or as the Merciful One) removes me farther from him and hinders me from drawing closer to him. Even the pronoun "he" diminishes my understanding of God

The mystery of God is that I can love truly — that is, more than myself or anything else — him alone. This love alone knows no bounds, no decrease (on the contrary, all is increase), no sensuality, no insincerity, no subservience, no fear, no self-satisfaction. Only through this love can I love all that is good. I can love and live only through him and by him.

For me, God is that eternal, infinite "not ourselves" that "makes for righteousness." God is not only the law of human life, but the inner motive that penetrates our being. God is love. Not love of wife, or child, or country, but of God — that very feeling of kindness, sympathy, and joy of life that constitutes our natural, blissful, true life, which knows no death.

II

Love is God. Therefore, love! Love even the one who has caused you pain, the one who is to blame. Then everything that conceals his soul from you will disappear, and you will, as through clear water, see at the bottom of his soul the divine essence of his love. And you will not have to, nor will you be able to, forgive him, for you will feel compelled to pardon only yourself for not having loved God in him, for not having seen God through the absence of your love.

Love is the manifestation within oneself of God. It is the propensity to get beyond oneself, to liberate oneself by living a God-centered existence. This very propensity calls forth God — that is, love for and in others. For love evokes love in others. God, having awakened in me, also produces the awakening of the same God in others.

III

To imagine a God-Creator is not only unnecessary but contrary to the Christian conception of God as Father and Spirit — the

God who is Love, a particle of whom lives in me and constitutes my life, the manifestation and avocation of which particle constitutes the meaning of my life.

A Creator-God doesn't exist. Such a god is indifferent and silently allows suffering and evil. But God the Spirit delivers us from suffering and evil, and is always perfect goodness. For God is Love, and if he is not perfectly, infinitely good he does not exist. Only the Father-God is; he alone is the origin of my spiritual self. It is to him we are to bow down.

IV

We cannot always be aware of the God who is living in us and acting through us. Some activities, for instance, demand our entire attention, and to think of God then would be unnecessary, even a distraction. The moment, however, we find in ourselves the seed of doubt, despondency, fear, and ill-will, we need to turn from whatever we are doing to God. We do this not to escape the work of life, but to gather strength for its accomplishment, for the victory over, the mastering of whatever hinders our communion with him. Like a bird — to advance on one's legs with folded wings, but the moment an obstacle is encountered, then to unfold one's wings and fly up. Then one finds relief, and one's burden disappears.

V

Once God becomes familiar to us we no longer really believe in him. Only when God discloses himself anew to us do we believe in him wholeheartedly. And he reveals himself anew to us when we seek him heart and soul. And yet we should never go to God, as it were, "on purpose." "Now let me just go to God. I will begin to live for God. Though I have been living solely for myself, I will now try and live for God."

There is harm in this, very great harm. It is a hundred times better to get well scalded against the devil than to continually stand at the crossroads, or insincerely go to God. Coming to God is something like getting married: one should come to God only when one would be glad not to come to him, or not to get married, but cannot help doing so. I can only come to God because I am compelled to do so.

VI

There are two distinct and mutually contradictory understandings of existence. The agnostic asserts that he can justifiably know nothing beyond what his empirical experience delivers. The believer, by contrast, begins with God in order to grasp his own existence.

For the agnostic, we are but mere animals and subject only to external sensations. Hence, we cannot rationally admit a spiritual origin, and so must resign ourselves to the senselessness of an existence that violates the demands of reason. For the believer, we are inherently rational creatures and thus deny the adequacy of the data of external or empirical experience. By itself, such data is as fantastic as it is erroneous.

From their respective starting points, both are right. But the difference between the agnostic and the believer is an essential one. For the agnostic, everything in the universe is strictly causal — a long flow of causes and effects that are rationally discernable — except the meaning of life itself! Neither we nor the universe have any discernable meaning. And so we are left without any overarching guidance in life. But for the person of faith, our lives, along with the universe itself, possess a definite, rational meaning. There exists a direct, simple, and universally accessible purpose for living, even if it transcends the dictates of science.

Who, I ask, is the more honest? *— Thoughts on God*

WHAT I BELIEVE

I believe in God, whom I understand as Spirit, as Love, as the Source of all. I believe that he is in me and I in him. I believe that the will of God is most clearly and intelligibly expressed in the teachings of the man Jesus, whom to consider a god that one is to pray to, I esteem the greatest blasphemy.

I believe that our true welfare lies in fulfilling God's will, and his will is that we should love one another and thus do unto others as we wish others to do to us. Therefore, I believe that the meaning of life consists in increasing the love that is in us; that this increase of love leads us, even in this life, to ever greater and greater happiness, and after death gives us the more happiness the more love we have, and helps more than anything else toward the establishment of God's kingdom on earth: that is, to the establishment of an order of life in which the discord, deception, and violence that now rule our world will be replaced by free accord, by truth, and by the brotherly love of one for another.

I believe there is only one means to obtain progress in love: prayer — not public prayer in churches, plainly forbidden by Jesus, but private prayer, like the one Jesus gave us. This kind of prayer alone renews and strengthens our awareness of life's meaning; it leads us to a complete dependence on God.

Whether or not these beliefs of mine offend, grieve, or prove a stumbling-block to anyone, or hinder anything, or give displeasure to anybody, I can as little change them as I can change my body. I must myself live my own life and I must alone meet death (and that very soon), and therefore I cannot believe otherwise than as I do believe.

I do not believe that my faith is an indubitable one — the Truth for all time. But I see no other faith that is simpler, clearer, or answers better all the demands of my mind and heart. Should I find a truer faith I shall at once accept it, for God requires nothing but the truth. "He who begins by loving Christianity better than truth will proceed by loving his own sect or church better than Christianity, and end in loving himself (his own peace) better than all," said Coleridge.

I have traveled the contrary way. I began by loving my Orthodox faith more than my peace, then I loved Christianity more than my church, and now I love truth more than anything in the world. And up to now truth for me is revealed in Christ and in his teachings, as I understand them. And I hold to this Christ, and to the degree in which I hold to his teachings I live peacefully and happily, and peacefully and happily approach death.

— Selected Essays

HELP MY UNBELIEF?

A person is sinking and asks to be saved; a rope is thrown out to him and the drowning man says, "Confirm my faith that the rope will save me. I believe," he says, "that the rope will save me, but help my unbelief." What does this mean? If that person does not seize the thing that can save him it only means that he does not understand his position.

How can a Christian, believing in Christ and all that he taught, say that he wishes to believe but cannot? Did not Christ say: You have before you everlasting torment, fire, infernal darkness — but here is your salvation! It is impossible not to believe in the offered salvation, not to fulfill it, and to say, "Help my unbelief." In order for someone to say this he must actually disbelieve in his own destruction and believe that he will not perish.

Children jump from a ship into the water. They are still upheld by the current, by their clothes, which are not yet soaked, and by their own feeble movements, and they do not understand their peril. From above, from the departing ship, a rope is thrown to them, they are told that they will certainly perish, and those on the ship beg them to save themselves. But the children do not believe. They disbelieve, not in the rope but in the fact that they are perishing. Other frivolous children like themselves have assured them that they will always continue merrily bathing even after the ship has gone. They do not believe that their clothes will soon be soaked, that their little arms will get tired, that they will begin to gasp, will be choked, and will go to the bottom. They do not believe in all this — solely because they do not see how they are in peril.

So it is with us. And so we cry out: "Confirm in us the belief that we are not perishing."

But this it is impossible to do! In order that we should have faith that we will not perish we must cease to do the things that destroy us and must begin to do the things that will save us — we must reach for the rope! But we don't want to do this and instead spend time assuring ourselves that we are not in danger, despite the fact that one after another of our comrades perishes before our very eyes. Yes, we believe, but not in what is true. All the while we cry out, "Help my unbelief."

— *What I Believe*

WHAT SIZE IS YOUR STONE?

Two women seeking wisdom went to a holy man. One of them considered herself a big sinner. She never stopped blaming herself for having betrayed her husband when she was young. The other had lived her whole life in accordance with God's commandments. Therefore, she did not reproach herself for having committed any particular sin and felt relatively good about herself.

The holy man questioned both of them about their lives. The first woman tearfully confessed her sin, huge at it was. She considered the sin so big that she did not expect to be forgiven. But out of desperation, she spoke it out anyway. The second woman said that she could not think of any particular sins she had committed, at least not any worth mentioning.

The holy man told the first woman, "Go, servant of God, beyond the city walls and find the largest stone you can carry and bring it to me." He said to the second woman, who was unaware of any particular sin, "Bring me stones also, but small ones, as many as you can carry." The women departed and carried out the holy man's command.

The first woman brought him a large stone, and the second woman, a sack full of small stones. The holy man looked at the stones and said, "Now here is what I want you to do. Take the stones back and put them in the same place where you found them. Then come back to me." The women went to fulfill the holy man's command.

The first woman easily found the place where she had gotten the stone and put it back where it was. The second woman could not remember where she had gotten all the little stones and therefore returned with a full sack to the holy man. The holy man told the first woman, "You easily returned the big, heavy stone, because you remembered where you got it." But to the second woman, he said: "You could not return the small stones, because you could not remember where you got them."

So it is with sin. The holy man said to the first woman, "You remembered your sin. Because of it you felt the pangs of your own conscience, and how your sin hurt others. Therefore you repented and in repenting you freed yourself of the burden of your sin." He said to the second woman, "You, however, tried returning small stones. Because you committed small sins, thinking little of them, you could not remember them.

Therefore, you could not repent of them. Instead, you learned to condemn the sins of others, like that of this other woman, while sinking deeper and deeper into your own. Certainly, your burden is far heavier."   — *Path of Life*

WHAT THEN IS PRAYER?

Jesus taught us to go into our own room and lock the door. In other words, prayer is complete only when done in solitude. The essence of prayer consists of communing with the God who dwells within us. It means recognizing oneself as the slave of God, and testing oneself, one's actions and desires, according to the demands of him who dwells within us.

Such prayer is not an idle sentimentality or some feeling of excitement, such as is produced by public prayer with its accompaniments of music, singing, images, illuminations, and exhortations. Genuine prayer helps us toward life — in reforming and guiding it.

Such prayer is a confession — one that tests me and points me ahead in the right direction. Suppose I have been insulted and have a bad feeling toward the person who insulted me. Maybe I want to do something bad to him. Or perhaps I simply won't help him in some way or another. Or suppose my property has been stolen, or I have lost a loved one. What will happen if I cease living in accordance with my faith?

If I do not pray in the right way I will never be free of the bad feelings I have toward those who have insulted me. So also with the loss of property or of a loved one — they will poison my life. But if I test myself in prayer before my soul and before God, something can change. Everything will be turned around. I will judge *myself*, not my enemy, and will do good to him, not harm. Furthermore, I will accept my losses as a trial, and try to bear them humbly. In this I will find comfort, and will see my way more clearly. Instead of trying to conceal from myself the inconsistency between my life and my faith, I will strive in prayer and with repentance to bring them into harmony. Then I shall find peace and joy.

Of what should prayer ultimately consist? Jesus showed us how to pray. He reminded us of what is most essential, both concerning God's will and of our struggle against sin.

Our Father in heaven, hallowed be your name. And your name, O God, is love. For he who abides in love abides in you, and you in him. For no one has seen you, O God, but if we love one another then you abide in us and your love is fulfilled. If anyone says, "I love God," but hates his brother, he is a liar, for he that does not love his brother whom he sees, how can he love God whom he has not seen?

Your kingdom come. Above all else, O God, I will live under your rulership and righteousness and I will trust that you will give me everything I need. For your kingdom is within us.

Your will be done on earth as it is in heaven. Do I truly believe, O God, that I am in you and you in me? And do I believe that my life consists in furthering love? Do I ask, and do I remember that today I am alive, but tomorrow I may be dead? Is it true that I don't live for personal desires and human glory, but only to fulfill your will here on earth?

Give us this day our daily bread. My food, O God, consists in doing your will, and completing it. I want to deny myself, take up your cross daily and follow you. I will take your yoke upon me and learn of you, for you are meek and humble in heart, and I will find peace for my soul; for your yoke is easy and your burden is light.

And forgive us our sins as we forgive those who sin against us. For you, Father, will not forgive me unless

I again and again forgive my brother who has sinned against me.

And lead us not into temptation. Help me, O God, to be on guard against the desires of the flesh: of ambition, of bitterness, of gluttony, adultery, human glory. Help my faith be sincere so that as I give alms my right hand won't know what my left is doing. For no one is fit for your kingdom if, after taking the plow, he looks back.

But deliver us from evil. Help me, O God, to become free of all that issues from my heart: evil thoughts, murder, envy, hate, theft, adultery (even in thought), deception, slander.

In the end, true solitary prayer brings the soul back to the consciousness of its divine source, to a more vivid and clear expression of the demands of our conscience, i.e., of our divine nature. Prayer tests our actions according to the highest demands of the soul. It keeps us honest, both with ourselves and with God.   — *On Reason, Faith, and Prayer*

THE NEED TO PRAY

Every day I feel the need to pray, to ask God for help. This need is natural (to us, at least, accustomed to it from childhood), perhaps natural to all people. To feel one's weakness and to seek help from outside oneself, i.e. not simply by struggling against evil but seeking ways to overcome evil — one feels the need to pray.

To pray, however, isn't a means of delivering us from evil. No. The various methods that deliver us from evil are themselves the act that we call prayer. The special thing about prayer is that, unlike other actions, it is in itself pleasing to God. It therefore does not have to be expressed only through words or rituals or other things of short duration, as is usually understood. Why can't prayer be expressed through prolonged actions of the arms and legs (isn't the journeying of pilgrims prayer by legs)? If I go and work a whole day or a week for a widow, is this not prayer?

Prayer is a request to grant some wish, inner or outer. I ask that my children shouldn't suffer or that I should be rid of my vice, my weakness. But why do I so quickly turn to some great and incomprehensible God with my requests when they can usually be fulfilled by people and by me?

I am weak, I am sinful, I have a vice (this is not an illustration but the truth; I have a terrible vice), which I am struggling against. I want to pray and do so in words. But isn't it better for me to broaden my understanding of prayer; isn't it better for me to seek the cause of this vice and find a divine activity, not of an hour's duration, but of days and months, a "prayerful" activity that could overcome this vice? I am sensual and I lead an idle, well-fed life, and I pray. Isn't it better for me to change my godless life, serve others, and cast away all the various means I use to satisfy my fleshly desires? If I do this, my whole life will become a prayer, and this prayer will surely be granted.

Does this mean that praying to God is a bad thing? Of course not! What is important, however, is to fulfill all that God requires of me, and for which he has given me the tools. And so if I have the means of saving myself with the aid of certain actions, or with the aid of other people, and I do nothing about it, and then pray to God, I should feel that I have done wrong.

I once fell into the temptation of lust. I suffered terribly, struggled, and felt my own powerlessness. I prayed and still felt I was powerless. I knew that I would fall at the first opportunity. Finally I performed a most loathsome act. I made an appointment with a woman, and was on my way to keep it. The same day I should have been giving a lesson to my second son. I walked past his window into the garden, and suddenly — something that had never happened before — he hailed me and reminded me that it was his lesson that day. Immediately, I came to my senses and didn't keep the appointment. Surely God saved me.

And God really did save me! But did the temptation pass after that? No, it remained, and I again felt that I would certainly fall. I then confessed my struggle to the teacher who was living with us and told him not to leave me at a certain time, and to help me. He was a good man. He understood me and looked after me like a child. Then later I took measures to have the woman moved elsewhere and I saved myself from sin, not in thought but in the flesh, and I know that that was right. Was it prayer that saved me?

A person who indeed loves God prays, but if I love God, then I consider him to be loving and good. If he loves me, he will save me and do everything I need, just as he made my son look out of the window. What am I to ask him for? It's like a child asking for soup, when his mother isn't giving it to him because she's blowing on the spoon.   — *Tolstoy's Letters*

THAT LITTLE CUP OF OIL

A monk was seeking salvation in the wilderness. He continually read his prayers and even got up twice a night to do so. A peasant used to bring him food. The monk started to wonder whether his way of life was holy enough, so he went to the saintly elder monk for guidance. He told the elder monk about his life, his way of praying, the words of his prayers, his getting up at night to pray, and his being fed by charitable offerings. He asked whether he was living right.

"All this is fine," said the elder monk, "but go and see how the peasant who feeds you lives. Maybe you can learn something from him."

The monk visited the peasant and spent a day and night with him. The peasant got up early and said only, "Lord." He went to work and plowed the fields the whole day. At night he came home and again said, "Lord." Then he lay down to sleep. The monk thought, "There is nothing I can learn here," and wondered why the elder monk had sent him to the peasant.

He returned to the elder monk and told him, "The peasant hardly thinks about God — he mentions Him only twice a day."

So the elder monk told him, "Take this cup full of oil and walk around the village and come back here without spilling a drop." The monk did what he was told. When he returned, the elder monk asked him, "How many times did you think about God while you were carrying the cup?" The monk admitted that he did not think about God even once. He said, "I only thought about not spilling the oil."

The elder monk said, "That little cup of oil kept you so preoccupied that you did not remember God even once. But the peasant fed himself, his family, and you with his labor and care and still remembered God twice a day."   — *Path of Life*

ONLY YOUR WORK

A Boss had a hired hand living with him, and the hired hand saw the Boss several times a day. The hired hand began to slack off and finally got so lazy that he was not doing anything. The Boss saw what was going on but did not say anything. He only turned away from the hired hand when he met him.

The hired hand realized the Boss was dissatisfied with him and tried to think of a way to placate him — but without having to do any work. So he went to the Boss's friends and acquaintances and asked them to ask the Boss not to be angry with him. The Boss found out about this, summoned the hired hand, and said: "Why are you asking my friends to put in a word for you? You are with me all the time. Why don't you tell me yourself what you need?" The hired hand did not know what to say, so he left.

Then the hired hand got another idea. He collected the Boss's chicken and eggs as presents and took them to him, so that the Boss would stop being angry with him. The Boss snapped back: "First you get my friends to speak for you, when you could speak directly to me yourself. Then you try to butter me up with presents, when, in fact, everything you have given me is mine already. If you only bring me what is mine, I do not need your presents."

Then the hired hand came up with yet another idea. He wrote songs praising the Boss and went back and forth past his window loudly singing and proclaiming that the Boss was a great and a kind and benevolent master. The Boss beckoned the hired hand to him again and said: "First you tried to gain my favor through intermediaries, then you gave me my own property as an offering, now you have thought up something even stranger: you are shouting and singing about me, saying I am so great and merciful, and so forth. You are exclaiming that I am this and I am that, but you do not even know me, and you do not want to know me either. I do not need your efforts to approach me through other people, nor your presents, nor your praise. I only need your work!"

We pray to saints asking them to intercede for us to God. We try to please God with all our candles, sanctuaries, tapestries, and singing to him our praises. But Jesus said: "If you love me, you will obey my commandments." Why do we do everything else but this? —*Path of Life*

TWO WAYS

There are two approaches in showing the way to a traveler. The same holds true for giving moral guidance. The first is to provide landmarks that one will meet on the road. The second is simply to give a person a bearing on a compass. On it the traveler will be able to make out an unchanging direction.

The first approach offers external rules: one is simply told which way to turn and which way to go, whether he knows where he is at or not. "Go to church," "Do not steal," "Do not kill," "Give to the poor," "Do not commit adultery," "Wash and pray five times a day," "Make the sign of the cross," and so on.

The second way — the way of Christ — points us to perfection, enabling us to strive toward that which we know to be true deep within ourselves. Knowing the ideal, we are able to detect any deviation from it. "Love the Lord your God with all your heart, with all your soul, with all your mind, with all your strength, and love your neighbor as yourself.... Be perfect as your heavenly Father is perfect."

In following external rules we need only to conform. Following Christ's teachings, however, demands that we are conscious of how far we are from attaining perfection. Though we are unable to know how close we are to this perfection, we can easily notice the extent of our deviation.

To follow mere rules is like someone standing in the light of a lamp fixed to a post. It is light all round him, but there is nowhere further for him to walk. To do Christ's will, by contrast, is like a person carrying a lantern on a pole: the light is in front of him, always lighting up fresh ground and always encouraging him to walk further ahead, even if what's ahead cannot be seen.

The Pharisee thanks God that he himself fulfills the law. He feels justified. The rich young man too was pleased that he had fulfilled the law since childhood. Neither the Pharisee nor the young man, however, were able to grasp what it was they were still lacking. And it is impossible for either of them to think otherwise: there is nothing ahead of them to which they could aspire. Tithes have been paid, Sabbaths observed, parents honored, robbery, adultery, murder have been avoided. What else is there?

One who follows Christ feels quite differently. He is in the position of the publican. He feels himself to be imperfect, unaware of the path he has traveled, and aware only of the path ahead he has yet to travel.

This is the difference between Christ's way and that of every other religion. Christ never laid down rules of conduct. He established no institutions, not even that of marriage. If only the Christian church understood how contrary its foundation is to the spirit of Christ and how it has supplanted the true ideal.

The so-called Christian teachings of the church have actually replaced Christ's original will. It is asserted that the Christian ideal is unattainable and thus cannot provide any genuine guidance for life. We can think and dream about it, but it is not applicable to life itself. What we need, therefore, is not an ideal but a rule, a means of guidance suited to our current situation and to the moral average of our society: if not a "proper" church wedding, then a civil marriage of some kind. Or even brothels. Why not? Brothels are indeed said to be preferable to prostitution on the streets.

And this is our problem. Once we allow ourselves to adapt the ideal to our own weakness, to our own perceived needs, it is impossible to define a boundary at which we must stop. But this whole line of reasoning is fundamentally flawed. Why do we have to conclude that the ideal of perfection cannot be a means of guidance in life? Why must we either throw it away, saying that it is unattainable and useless, or else lower it to a level that is adapted to our own weakness?

It is as though a sailor were to say: "Since I cannot keep to the bearing indicated by my compass, I must either stop looking at the compass or even throw it out (i.e., abandon the ideal), or else fasten the compass needle so that it points out the direction in which my ship is traveling at the given moment (i.e., adapt the ideal to my own weakness)." Christ's way is not a dream, neither is his teaching a rhetorical exhortation. It is the most indispensable and accessible form of moral guidance there is—

just as the compass is the most important and useful instrument of guidance for a sailor.

"But we are weak, we must have a goal within reach of our powers," people say. That is like saying, "My hands are weak and I cannot draw a straight line. In order to make things easier, I shall take a crooked and broken line as my model." The weaker my hand, the greater my need of a perfect model.

The main thing is to not be afraid to define precisely one's deviation from the ideal direction. Whatever position we may have reached, it is always possible for us to draw nearer to the ideal. We can never say that we have attained it or that we cannot aspire further. We may believe that rules are more easily realized, and that without them we shall lapse into depravity. But this is little more than a ploy to cover up our lack of faith in the ideal and our refusal to regulate our lives according to it.

While a sailor keeps near the coast, one can say: "Steer by that cliff, that cape, that tower." But there comes a time when far from shore the only possible guidance is from the unattainable heavenly luminaries and the compass indicating a direction. Both of these have been given to us.

— Afterword to *Kreutzer Sonata*

THE STEEP SLOPE OF DESIRE

In our society, children are seen either as an obstacle to pleasure, an unfortunate accident, or — if only a prearranged number are born — as a kind of pleasure in themselves. For this reason, they are not brought up to discover their task in life, as being capable of reason and love. They are brought up more like the young of animals.

The main concern of parents, a concern exacerbated by false educational theories and expectations, is not to prepare their children for activities worthy of human beings, but to feed and dress them as well as possible and make them grow quickly, have them clean, white, good-looking, safe, and comfortable. And these children, like over-fed animals, develop an overpowering sensuousness, which results in a great deal of confusion and suffering as adolescents. Their whole environment, their clothes, their books, their music, their dances, their food — everything from the pictures on boxes to novels, stories, and plays, comes together to inflame a life given to the flesh.

This is why the young people of our day are in a very precarious situation. The danger lies in the fact that at an age when habits are formed which, like folds on a sheet of paper, will remain forever, the young live their lives without the slightest moral or spiritual restraint. Aware of the oppressive "moral code" that is forced upon them by "society," which they try in one way or another to escape, they give themselves to a plethora of pleasures that tempt them on all sides and that society gives them the opportunity to enjoy.

Though this situation appears to be quite natural and normal, it is something appallingly dangerous. It is dangerous because when our desires are new and especially powerful, as they are in youth, our aim in life soon becomes the enjoyment and satisfaction of these desires — whether of good food, sports, fine clothes, or music. But with this comes the incessant want and need for more. One is never content and not only thirsts for a second or a third indulgence of identical pleasure but for new and stronger pleasures. (There is even a mathematical law according to which the degree of pleasure increases in arithmetical progression, while the means for producing this pleasure increase in geometrical progression.)

This is always how it goes: candy, flavored drinks, bicycles and horses; then steak, cheese, alcohol, tobacco, fashion, and the opposite sex. And since sexual lust is the strongest of all lusts, expressed variously through falling in love, caresses, masturbation, and intercourse, it never takes very long before a young person reaches this stage. Lastly, when it is no longer possible to replace these pleasures with anything new and more potent, one reaches the stage of relying on artificially exaggerated pleasures through self-intoxication, drugs, pulsating music, and other means of stimulation and excitement.

This path is so common today that few young people reach adulthood unscathed; some are entirely destroyed. Rich or poor, this is what young people confront. However, it is especially bad for those who are well off, since they are in a position of being able to satisfy their lusts more quickly, and so more quickly grow bored and grasp after extremes.

If young people, especially, would only grasp how disastrous it is to pursue earthly treasures! Like moths attracted to a flame, the young indulge the senses, mercilessly trampling on and destroying the good in them. They live without any definite direction to their life except that in which they are drawn — here today, there tomorrow — by their whims and desires. Is this really any way to live?

Christ surely points us to a different way, indicating a path that is joyful to follow but disastrous if not. He has warned us against false joys and pleasures, snares and temptations. He delineated them in detail, cautioned us against them, showed us the ways of escaping from them, and promised us greater joys — along with true happiness — in exchange. He directs us toward a purpose outside of ourselves, one based on the highest good. He has given us simple instructions, which, if followed, will deliver us from emptiness.

Christ especially warns against the pursuit of pleasure. As bodily beings, we will always seek to satisfy our physical desires. The temptation, however, is to believe that such satisfaction brings happiness. The satisfaction of our desires, especially at the expense of others, along with every satisfaction of lust, brings in its train an inevitable and a countless number of new lusts — desires that are even more difficult to satisfy, and so on *ad infinitum*. Herein lies the snare, which, always leads to torment.

We have been given the joy of good food, the joy of an appetite developed by labor and self-restraint. A crust of bread, if one is hungry, can be eaten with more pleasure than pineapples and truffles when one is not. And yet we have now arranged our life so comfortably that we are hardly ever hungry. We have spoiled our appetite with such lavishly flavored food that when we eat it we receive little or no pleasure from it, suffering instead from indigestion, stomach pains, and flabbiness.

We forget that we have been given the pleasure, yes pleasure, of exercising our muscles in work and the joys of rest that follow, and yet we make other people or machines work for us, depriving ourselves of real satisfaction.

We've been given the happiness of associating with other people, of friendship and community, and yet, instead of enjoying these, we set ourselves apart from everyone else and limit our dealings to a small circle of people who for the most part are just as off base as we are. We've been given the enormous happiness of family love, and yet we squander this happiness through infidelity and the pursuit of material security.

We wish for peace and rest and so look for ways of avoiding physical and mental work. In the process we lose the skill and ability to sweat hard and, inadvertently, lose the ability to rest well. We wish for the joys of sexual love and yet destroy the possibility of this love when the right time for it arises.

Only two paths are available: the path of subordinating our earthly wants to spiritual ideals, which lead to genuine, eternal joy, or the path of temporal, fleeting joys based on immediate, physical pleasures. This latter path leads to disaster. It not only deprives us of the awareness of eternal life, but of the life-giving joy God wants to give us here and now while we are on this earth. — *Tolstoy's Letters*

WHAT IS MARRIAGE FOR?

To marry in order to enjoy life more will never work. To place marriage — union with the person you love — as your main aim is a big mistake. And it's obvious if you think about it.

The aim is marriage. Well, you get married, and then what? If you have no other goal in life before marriage, then later on it will be extremely difficult, almost impossible for the two of you, to find one. It's almost certain that if you have no common aim before marriage, nothing will bring you together afterward, and you will have one falling out after another. Marriage only brings happiness when there is a single aim beyond itself, when people meet on the road and say, "Let's walk together — yes let's!" and offer one another their hands — and not when people are attracted to one another and then both turn off the road in different directions.

Life is neither a vale of tears nor a circus of entertainment. Life is essentially a place of service, where on occasion one has to put up with a lot that is difficult, but more often than not where one can experience a great many joys. But real joy is had only when we see our life as service. Usually married people forget this completely.

Marriage and the birth of children offer so many enjoyable experiences that it seems that these things actually constitute life itself. But this is a dangerous delusion. If parents live and have children without also having a life purpose, there will be nothing to point their children to or guide them along the way. And then they will lose their human qualities as children and the happiness linked with them, and become pedigree cattle.

Those intending to marry, even if their life seems full, need more than ever to think and make clear to themselves what it is they are living for. And in order to do this, it's necessary to think, and to think hard about the conditions one lives in and about one's past, to evaluate what one considers to be important and unimportant in life and to find out what one really believes in — i.e., what one considers the invariable, indisputable truth, and what one will be guided by in life. And not only find out and make clear to oneself, but experience it in practice and put it into deeds. Otherwise, one does not truly know what he believes in, or whether one believes it or not.

If life is service, then the "good" consists of love. In order to love I must first train myself to require as little from others as possible. Unless I do this, I will be inclined not to love but to reproach. This demands a lot of work. Second, in order to love I must do something useful for others. This involves even more work. Lastly, it is necessary to learn gentleness, humility, and the art of enduring unpleasant people and unpleasant things, and whenever possible to never offend. This requires the most work of all, and work that is nonstop, from waking up to going to sleep. But this is the most joyful sort of work.

When considering marriage, therefore, a couple needs to think and live as lovingly as possible so that they can find out whether they are really going along the same road and whether or not it's good for them to give each other the hand. If they are sincere, the thought of marriage will lead them to what is higher, to find ways to bring more love and truth into the world. They will marry because it will enable them to attain this aim. But once having chosen what is higher, it will be necessary for them to put their whole heart and soul into it, not just a little bit of oneself; a little bit is no use!   — *Tolstoy's Letters*

THE HAPPINESS OF LOVE

We know that in addition to the satisfaction of our bodily wants there is a better, fuller happiness, one that becomes all the greater in proportion to the renunciation of our own personal well-being. It is a feeling that solves all the contradictions of human life. It is love.

Love alone is the only reasonable activity or pursuit of humankind. Like a key made for this one lock alone, we find in our own soul a feeling that gives us what it is we yearn for. And this feeling not only solves the riddles of life, but finds in them the very possibility of happiness. For love not only annihilates our fear of meaninglessness but empowers us to seek the happiness of others. And this indeed is our greatest happiness.

Love is more than a feeling. It is an activity directed toward the well-being of others. It is also indiscriminate, and it does not proceed in any definite order. The demands of love present themselves constantly, all at once, without any hierarchy. Just now a hungry old man, of whom I am rather fond, comes to me and asks for the food I am keeping for the supper of my dearly loved children. How can I weigh the demands of a temporary and less powerful love with the future demands of a stronger love?

A lawyer put these same questions to Christ: "Who is my neighbor?" In fact, how are we to decide whom to serve, and in what degree? People or our fatherland? Our fatherland or our friends? Our friends or our wife? Our wife or our father? Our father or our children? Our children or ourselves?

Love demands a response in each of these relationships, but all of these relationships are so interwoven with each other that the satisfaction of the demands of some deprives us of the possibility of satisfying the demands of the others. If I say it is possible not to clothe a shivering child because some day my children will suffer as a result, then, in the name of my future children, why should I yield to other demands of love?

It is precisely the same in relation to love for one's country, for chosen occupations, and for all people. If we can neglect the demands of the very smallest love here and now, in the name of the very greatest love in the future, is it not clear that we, even if we desire this with all our hearts, will never be in a condition to properly determine how to love? In other words, won't we always choose the manifestation of love that is most agreeable to us, and act, not in the name of love, but in the name of our individuality? If we decide that it is better for us to refrain from the demands of the smallest love in the here and now in the name of a future and different manifestation of a greater love, then we deceive either ourselves or others, and love no one but ourselves.

There is no love in the future. Love is activity in the present. And the person who manifests no love in the present has no love.

What most of us call love is only the familiar preference of our personal happiness to others. When we say that we love our wife or child or friend, we merely say that these are the people who heighten our personal happiness.

If we were but animals without reason, we would love those whom we do love, our wolf-cubs, our flock. And we would not know that we love our wolf-cubs or our flock, and we would not know that other wolves love their cubs, and other flocks their comrades in the flock, and their love would be that love and that life which are possible on that plane of consciousness upon which they find themselves.

But we are beings with conscience and thus cannot help seeing that others cherish the same love for their own as we do for ours. Our feelings of love will invariably come into conflict with that of others, creating quite the opposite of what love demands.

Genuine love is actually a preference of other beings to one's self. Real love always has as its foundation the renunciation of individual happiness and the affection toward all people that arises therefrom. Only upon this universal affection can spring up genuine love for particular people — one's own relatives or strangers. And such love not only gives the true bliss of life, but solves the apparent contradictions of our life.   *— On Life*

CHRISTIAN FREEDOM

One of the most striking phenomena of our times is how slavery, in the name of freedom, continues to be perpetrated, especially among those advocating theories of social change. These people argue that the amelioration of life will come, not as the result of the personal resolve of individuals, but of itself as the result of certain institutions. It's as if we are meant to walk on our own legs but that a kind of floor under our feet will somehow be moved, so that on it we can reach where it is we ought to go, but without moving our own legs. And so today all our efforts are supposed to be directed, not to going as far as our strength allows in the direction we ought to go, but to standing still and constructing such a floor.

We are like a swarm of bees hanging in a cluster to a branch. The position of the bees on the branch is temporary and must inevitably be changed. They must start off and find themselves a habitation. Each of the bees knows this and desires to change its own and the others' position, but no one of them can do it until the rest of them do it. They cannot all start off at once, because one hangs on to another and hinders it from separating from the swarm, and therefore they all continue to hang there. It would seem that the bees could never escape from their position, just as it seems that we today, caught in the toils of fending for ourselves, can never escape. And there would be no escape for the bees, if each of them were not a living, distinct creature, endowed with wings of its own. Similarly there would be no escape for us if we were not each a living being endowed with a conscience in communion with God.

If every bee that could fly did not try to fly, the others too would never be stirred, and the swarm would never change its position. And if the person who has mastered the Christian conception of life would not, without waiting for other people, begin to live in accordance with this conception, the rest of us would never change position. But let only one bee spread its wings, start off and fly away, and after it another, and another, and the clinging, inert cluster would become a freely flying swarm of bees. Just in the same way, only let one person look at life as Christ teaches us to look at it, and after him let another and another do the same, and the enchanted circle of existence of selfish pursuits, from which there seems no escape, will be broken through.

Tragically, most of us think that to set people free by this means is too slow a process and thus must find some other way. It's as if the bees who wanted to fly away should consider it too long a process to wait for all the swarm to start one by one. Instead, they think there ought to be some other way so that it wouldn't be necessary for every single bee to spread its wings and fly off — a way in which the whole swarm could fly at once where it wanted to. But that is not possible. Only until a first, a second, a third, a hundredth bee spreads its wings and flies off of its own accord will the swarm fly off and begin its new life. Only when every individual person makes Christ's teachings his own, and begins to live as Christ did, can there be a solution to the problem of human life, and to the establishment of a new way to live.   — *The Kingdom of God Is within You*

THE MORAL KNIFE

Most of us assume that morality is a very insipid and vague affair, in which little new or helpful can be discerned with regards to the complicated world of political, scientific, cultural, and commercial activity. Yet nothing is farther from the truth. These spheres of activity have no other object than to elucidate moral truths and to confirm, simplify, and make them accessible to all.

Once while I was walking on a street in Moscow I saw a man engrossed in examining the flagstones. Choosing one of them, he sat down and began to scrape and rub it vigorously.

"What is he doing with the pavement?" I wondered. And, having come up close to him, I discovered he was a young man from a butcher's shop, and he was sharpening his knife on the flagstone. He was not thinking about the stones at all, and still less when busy at his work. He was interested only in cutting meat, though at first I thought he was trying to do something to the pavement.

Similarly, as we go about our commercial and cultural activities, the most important thing to keep in mind is to elucidate those moral truths that are necessary to live by.

Moral laws exist; we have only to rediscover them. Elucidating them may appear unimportant and imperceptible to the one who sees no need of moral guidance. Yet this is not only the most important, but ought to be the sole business of everyone. This elucidation is imperceptible in the same way as the difference between a sharp knife and a blunt one is imperceptible. A knife remains a knife. And if you don't have anything to cut you will not notice its edge. But if you grasp that your very life depends on whether your knife is blunt or sharp, every improvement in sharpening it is important. You know good and well that a knife is a knife only when it is sharp, and when it cuts what it has to cut.   — *What Is to Be Done?*

Maxims and Musings

SEEKING TRUTH

Happiness lies in the search for truth, not in finding it.

•

When people tell you that you will never be able to know the truth, because the whole truth can never be found, do not believe them for a minute. Be wary of such people! They are not only the enemies of truth, they are *your* enemies. They talk this way because they do not live their lives according to the truth, and thus want others to live like they do.

•

In order to understand the truth don't suppress your intellect, purify it.

•

Don't be fooled by those who speak badly about others but well of yourself.

•

Like fire, truth consumes all the disguises that hide it.

•

Don't be bothered by not knowing this or that. Be afraid of knowing what is useless. It is better to know less than you could than to know more than you need to know. Knowing "too much" makes you more stupid than if you had never learned anything.

•

Those who stand at the top find it most difficult to understand what is required of them. They become giddy from the height of the structure of lies on which they stand when they look at the spot on the earth to which they must descend in order to begin to live, not righteously, but only not quite inhumanly. And this is why the plain and clear truth appears to them so strange.

•

A genuine thinker or artist will never sit on the heights of Olympus, as we are apt to imagine. He must suffer in company with his fellow humans. He will suffer because he is anxious to find out and tell others what he has discovered about happiness and what it is that might save us from our misery. He is especially anxious because he knows that tomorrow may be too late. Suffering and self-sacrifice is thus the true lot of any thinker and artist.

•

The concept of a church as a gathering of "elect" — of "better" people — is a proud, false concept that is not Christian. Who is better? Who is worse? Peter was "better" until the cock crowed, and the robber was "worse" until he hung on the cross. Haven't we encountered in ourselves an angel and a devil both of whom are so intertwined that we cannot completely rout the angel nor prevent the devil from peeping around? How can we, such mixed beings as we are, consider ourselves to be the church consisting of the chosen or the righteous? There is the light of truth — and there are people who are approaching it from all sides — from as many angles as there are radii in a circle, in other words, by infinitely varied paths. Let us use all our strength to go toward the light that unites us all. How close we are to the light or how united we are is not for us to judge.

•

All great revolutions commence in thought. Let but a change take place in people's thoughts, and new deeds will follow, for action will follow the direction of thought as certainly as the ship follows the direction of the rudder.

•

A Christian knows the truth only in the sense that he shows it to others.

•

There is one thing, and only one thing, that enables us to be free in life; everything else is beyond our power: to recognize and profess the truth.

•

If we took any twig from a spreading bush it will be quite correct to say that from twig to branch, and from branch to limb, and from limb to trunk, every part is derived from the root, but none of them is exclusively so derived. To say of any particular twig that it is the only true twig would be absurd. Yet this is exactly what so many of our Christian churches say, that *their* faith is the only true one.

•

Why does the rising sun light up some objects before reaching others? The sun of truth rising higher and higher over the world lights up more and more of it, and is reflected first by those objects which are first reached by its illuminating rays and are best fitted to reflect them. But the qualities that make some people more suited to receive the rising truth are not any especially active qualities of mind, but are the passive qualities of heart, rarely coinciding with a great and inquisitive intellect, renunciation of the cares of the world, consciousness of one's own material insignificance, and great sincerity, as we see exemplified by all the founders of religion.

•

Christian truth has this peculiarity that if it is not embraced in its entirety, it may as well not be embraced at all.

RELIGION

It is terrible when people do not know God, but it is worse when people confuse God with what is not God.

•

If we are unaware that we are breathing air, we become aware of it as soon as the air is cut off and we begin to choke. We realize that there is something we cannot live without. The same thing happens to us when we lose our connection with God.

•

The principles of true religion are simple, universal, intelligible, and clear. There is a God, the origin of all that is; there dwells a spark from the Divine in each person, and this spark can increase or decrease depending on how we live; to increase this spark we must suppress our selfish wants and egos and grow in love; the practical means to attain love is to do to others what you would have them do to you.

•

There is a legend that tells of an angel who descended to earth and, entering the house of a devout family, slew a child in its cradle. When asked why he did so, he explained that the child would have become the greatest of malefactors and would have destroyed the happiness of the family. In the end, we cannot decide any of the most important questions of life by considerations of their immediate results or consequences. What then are we to do? We must integrate, that is to say, we must set up, besides our relation to the immediate facts of life, a relation to the whole immense Infinite in time and space conceived as one whole. We must draw guidance from the whole of which we feel a part.

FAITH

One of the most vulgar of all prejudices is the belief that we can live without faith.

•

Thinking that there is no God is like believing that if you blow air with a bellows, the air comes from the bellows and not from the air, and that the bellows would work even without air.

•

Can there be a more stupid idea than "proving" God? Being asked to prove God's existence is like being asked to prove the fact that we are alive. Prove to whom? How? Why? If there were no God, then there would be nothing. How, then, can you "prove" him?

•

The distance we have gone is less important than the direction in which we are going.

•

Live seeking God, then you will not live without God.

•

Pascal wrote: "There are only three kinds of people: first, those who find God and serve him; secondly, those who, not finding him, are occupied in the search for him; and thirdly, those who neither find him nor seek for him. The first are reasonable and happy; the last are unreasonable and unhappy; those in between are unhappy but reasonable."

The distinction, however, between those who find God and serve him, and those who, not finding him, still seek him with all their hearts, is not a very clear one. I think that those who with all their hearts and with agony seek God are already serving him. They are serving him by the fact that by these sufferings their searching traces out and opens the way for others to reach God. What better service is there?

•

We can understand the existence of God only when we feel our complete dependence on him, just like an infant feels when his mother holds him. A baby does not know who feeds him, who warms him, who takes care of him, but he understands that there *is* someone who does this, and thus loves the force in whose power he rests.

OBEDIENCE

There is the God that people in general believe in — the God who serves us (sometimes in very subtle ways, say, by merely giving us peace of mind). This God does not exist. The only God who exists is the one whom most of us forget — the God we are called to serve.

•

Suppose an architect says to a homeowner, "Your house is good for nothing; it must be completely rebuilt," and then gives details as to what beams should be cut, and how it should be done and where they should be placed. But then the owner turns a deaf ear to the architect's words, yet in the pretense of showing respect, heeds the architect's suggestions about how to arrange the rooms. Evidently, in this case, all the subsequent advice of the architect will seem to be impractical; a less respectful owner would regard it as nonsense.

But it is precisely in this way that we treat the teachings of Jesus. I give this illustration for want of a better. I remember now that Jesus made use of the same comparison. "Destroy this temple," he said, "and in three days I will raise it up." It was for this they put him on the cross, and for this they now crucify his teaching.

•

The church is not made up of those who say "Lord, Lord," and bring forth iniquity, but of those who hear the words of truth and reveal them in their lives. The members of this church practice the commandments of Jesus and thereby teach them to others. Whether this church be in numbers little or great, it is, nevertheless, the church that will never perish, the church that shall finally unite within its bonds the hearts of all mankind. "Fear not, little flock, for it is your Father's good purpose to give you the kingdom."

•

It is far easier to write ten volumes of philosophy that to put a single precept into practice.

•

How does a lapse of faith occur? Very simply: one begins to live like everybody else.

•

The most important acts are those that have remote consequences.

THE INNER LIFE

We can live for a hundred years without noticing that we have long been dead and have rotted away.

•

We say, "I know I should do more, but I can't on account of my current circumstances." This is not true! The inner work that is the essence of life can always be done. Whether you are in prison, or sick, or deprived for whatever reason, or whether you are being insulted or tortured — your inner life is under your control. In your thoughts you can blame, judge, envy, or hate others; or you can think good thoughts. The decision is yours.

•

We regret losing a purse or wallet full of money, but a good thought which has come to us, which we have either heard or

read, a thought which we should have remembered and applied
to our life, which could have improved the world — we lose this
thought and promptly forget about it, and we do not regret it,
though it is more precious than millions.

•

There is no such thing as a political change of the social system:
only moral change within the soul.

•

Dissatisfaction with oneself is a sign of friction, and therefore a
sign of movement.

•

We live badly, because we are bad. Therefore, if we want life to
stop being bad, we have to turn bad people into good people.
How do we do that? You cannot transform anyone but yourself. At first it seems that by doing this you will not change
anything. Who am I compared to so many? But we all com-
plain about how bad life has become. If we grasped that bad
people are what creates this bad life and that we cannot change
other people but can only work on changing ourselves, then life
would start to improve.

•

The state of the soul of the person who hates even one of his
brothers is terrible; but what must be the state of the soul of a
person who hates an entire class?

•

A river that is deep does not make waves when someone throws
a stone into it. The same applies with us. If you get angry at
insults thrown at you, you are a puddle.

CONSCIENCE

We spoil our lives more by doing what we should not do than by not doing what we should do. Our conscience always bothers us more for what we have done than for what we have failed to do.

•

It is better to cut your clothes to fit your conscience than to fit your body.

•

The conscience cannot be calmed by new ideas. No. It can be calmed only when we stop trying to justify ourselves.

•

We do not rock children in the cradle to eliminate the cause of their distress but simply to stop the crying. We do the same with our conscience, when we silence it to secure people's approval. We do not really quiet our conscience, but we do achieve our goal — we no longer hear its voice.

•

The same tragedy afflicts millions of people — not so much that they live bad lives as that they do not live in accord with their own conscience. People follow some other conscience instead of their own, perhaps some higher conscience. And then, since they are clearly incapable of living in accord with this other conscience, they end up following no conscience at all, neither this other conscience nor their own. All this is a great evil.

•

Two "persons" live in each and every individual. One person is blind and material; the other is perceptive and spiritual. One — the blind one — eats, drinks, works, rests, reproduces, and does everything as if according to a timetable. The other — the perceptive, spiritual person — does not do anything but only approves or disapproves of what the blind, "animal" side does.

We call the perceptive, spiritual side of a person "conscience." Conscience acts like the needle of a compass. A compass needle moves only when the person carrying it moves away from the path indicated by the needle. The same is true of conscience: it is quiet as long as we are doing what we should. As soon as we deviate from the right path, our conscience tells us where and how far we have strayed.

•

If I fall into the sea, it makes no difference into what sea I fall. Whether or not I can swim is all that matters. Power is not located outside us but in our ability to control ourselves.

•

Said the Christian Martyr, "I cannot kill. I cannot do what is opposed to the way of Christ."

"Then we will imprison you, and torture you to death."

"That is your business. You do your work and I will do mine."

•

There was once a Roman empress who lost her precious jewelry. It was announced that whoever found her lost stones within thirty days would receive a big reward, but anyone who returned the jewelry after thirty days would be executed. Samuel, a rabbi, found the precious stones, but he waited to return them until after thirty days had passed. "Have you been abroad?" the empress asked him. "No, I was at home." "Maybe you did not know what was proclaimed?" "No, I knew," said Samuel. "Then why did you not return these things before the thirty days were over? Now you have to be executed." "I wanted to show you that I returned your lost jewelry, not because of fear of your punishment, but because of fear of God."

SIN AND TEMPTATION

It is human to sin; it is diabolic to try to justify those sins.

•

Look within and you will invariably find the same sin you condemn in others. If you do not find the same sin, you only have to dig a little deeper to find a worse one.

•

It is bad when we live surrounded by sinful people and therefore cannot see either our own sins or the sins of others; but it is even worse when we see the sins of those around us but cannot see our own.

•

People are not punished "for" their sins but "by" their sins. This is the worst and truest punishment.

•

When we live bad lives we are apt to say that God does not exist, and we are right — God exists only for those who are looking in his direction and moving toward him. When we have turned away from God and are moving in the opposite direction from him, there is no God and there cannot be God.

•

The coachman does not throw down the reins just because the horses do not stop right away. No, he keeps tugging on the reins, and the horses eventually stop. Likewise, you will not control your passions right away but continue to struggle anyway. In the end, you, and not your passions, will win.

•

We would think a person insane who, instead of covering his house with a roof and putting windows in his window frames, goes out in stormy weather and scolds the wind, the rain, and the clouds. But we all do the same thing when we scold and blame the faults in other people instead of fighting the sin that exists in us.

•

The only person who doesn't fall is the one who doesn't strive toward anything. Fall a thousand times and get up a thousand times and if you don't despair, you will make progress.

•

Each sin begins to bind us immediately. The first time the bond is as thin as a spider web. If the sin is repeated, the spider web becomes a thread, then a string. If the sin continues to be repeated, it becomes a rope and finally a chain. At first sin is a stranger in your soul, then a friend. As soon as you get used to its presence, sin becomes the master of your soul.

•

A person whose shoes are clean steps carefully around the mud. After he steps in the mud, he is no longer so careful. After his shoes get covered in mud, he steps with abandon, dirtying his shoes even more. Likewise, when a person is still young and unstained by bad or dissolute deeds, he avoids evil and guards himself against doing anything bad. But as soon as he errs once or twice, he thinks, "No matter how hard I try, I fail anyway," and he throws himself into all sorts of vice. Do not do this. If you get dirty, wipe yourself off and be more careful — be sorry and then try again to avoid sin.

•

The habit of giving into our lusts is like a hidden stream under the foundations of a house. The house will eventually fall.

DOING GOOD

Before I try to do good, I must first leave off doing evil and put myself in a position in which I should cease to cause it. But my entire course of life is evil. If I were to give away a hundred thousand dollars, I have not yet put myself in a situation where I can do good, because I still have five hundred thousand left.

It is only when I possess nothing that I shall be able to do a little good, such as, for example, the poor prostitute did when she nursed a sick woman and her child for three days. Yet this seems to me to accomplish so little! And *I* venture to think I can do good!

•

The simplest and shortest rule of morality consists in compelling as little service as possible from others, and serving others as much as possible. It involves demanding as little as possible from others, and in giving others as much as possible.

•

If you cannot do unto others what you would have them do unto you, at least do not do unto them what you would not want them to do unto you. If you don't want to be made to work ten hours at a stretch, if you don't want your children hungry, cold, and ignorant, if you don't want to be robbed of the land that feeds you, if you don't want to be shut up in prisons and sentenced to death for committing some unlawful act in the heat of the moment, if you don't want to be killed or your home destroyed in war — do not do this to others. All this is so simple and straightforward that it is impossible for the simplest child not to understand, and for the most erudite person to refute.

COMPROMISE

A dead tree can stand as firmly as ever — it may even seem firmer because it is harder — but it is rotten at the core, and soon must fall. It is just so with the present order of society, based on force. It appears stronger than ever, with all its military arsenal, but it is on its way to collapse.

•

To put an engine in position, to heat the boiler, to set it in motion, but not to attach the connecting belt is what has been done with the teaching of Christ. People teach Christianity but don't practice it.

•

If the Gospels had been discovered half-burnt or obliterated it would have been easier to recover their meaning than it is now, when so many dishonest interpretations have been applied to them.

•

On the one hand we call ourselves Christians, professing the principles of liberty, equality, and fraternity. On the other, we are ready, in the name of liberty, to submit to the most asinine degradation. In the name of equality, we accept the crudest, most senseless division of people into higher and lower classes, allies and enemies; and, in the name of fraternity, we are ready to kill our brothers, even fellow Christians.

•

The fate of Christianity is astonishing! It has been made a domestic, pocket-sized affair, it's been rendered harmless, and people have accepted it in that form, and not only accepted it but grown used to it and settled down comfortably with it. And suddenly it starts to expand in all its enormous importance, terrifying them and shattering their orderly regime. Christ's life and death suddenly acquire their true, accusatory importance, and the people are terrified and shun it.

NONVIOLENCE

People long ago were unable to see that indulgences, inquisitions, slavery, and tortures were incompatible with Christianity. But a time came when they saw it as comprehensible. And a time will come when people will see Christian faith is incompatible with war service and of service to the government in general. Government is violence; Christ's way is meekness, nonresistance, love. It is that simple.

•

To destroy another life for the sake of justice is like repairing the misfortune of losing one arm by cutting off the other arm for the sake of equity.

•

Hunters used to kill bears by putting honey in a tub and then hanging a heavy log in a tree overhead. The bear pushes the log away to get at the honey, and the log swings back and knocks him down. The bear gets mad and hits the log harder — and is knocked down again harder. This goes on until the log kills the bear. We do the same thing whenever we return evil for evil. Can't we learn to be more rational than bears?

•

There is a hard and fast rule we must always remember: if a good end can be achieved only through bad means, either it is not a good end, or its time has not yet come.

•

The evil we use violence against to protect ourselves from is far less evil than the evil we do to ourselves by using violence.

•

Forcing people to stop behaving badly is like damming a river. Just as the river will eventually spill over the dam and flow the same way it always has, when we don't change from within we will eventually go on behaving as we always have before.

•

Punishing someone who has done something wrong is like
adding fuel to a fire. A person who has done something wrong
is already punished, because he loses his peace of mind and his
conscience bothers him. If his conscience does not bother him,
then all the punishment in the world will not change him — it
will only make him more bitter.

•

It is said that Christ's teaching is irrelevant to the complexities
of our industrial age. It is as if the existence of this industrial age
were a sacred fact. It is just as though drunkards when advised
how they could be brought to habits of sobriety should answer
that the advice is incompatible with their habit of taking alcohol. Christ's teaching is irrelevant because, if it were carried into
practice, life could not go on as at present.

•

People bound together by a delusion form, as it were, a col-
lective cohesive mass. The cohesion of that mass is the world's
evil. All revolutions are attempts to break up that mass, but by
violence. By breaking up the mass it appears that the mass will
cease, and therefore people strike it, but by trying to break it
they only forge it closer. The cohesion of the particles is not
destroyed until the inner force passes from the mass to the particles and obliges them to separate from it. The strength of that
cohesion of people lies in a falsehood, a fraud. The force freeing
each particle of the human cohesive mass is truth. We can pass
on the truth only by deeds of truth.

•

The use of force leads us to the fatal conviction that we progress, not through the spiritual impulse, which constitutes the
only source of every progressive movement of humanity, but
by means of violence, the very thing which, far from leading
us to truth, always carries us further away from it. This is a
fatal error, because it neglects the chief force underlying our
life — our spiritual activity — and turns all our attention and

energy to that which is superficial, sluggish, and most generally pernicious.

We make the same mistake as people who, trying to set a steam engine in motion, try and turn its wheels round with their hands, not suspecting that the underlying cause of its movement is the expansion of the steam, and not the motion of the wheels. By turning the wheels by hand and by levers they only produce a semblance of movement, and in so doing, they are wrenching the wheels and so preventing their being fit for real movement.

•

At first glance it appears that revolutionaries and Christians are the same: no state — no state; no property — no property; no inequality — no inequality; and much else. But not only is there a big difference, there are no people further apart. For a Christian there is no state, but for revolutionaries it is necessary to destroy the state; for a Christian there is no property, but the subversives destroy property. It's just like two ends of a ring that haven't been joined up. The ends are adjacent, but they are further apart from each other than all the other parts of the ring are. You have to go right round the ring in order to join up the ends.

WAR

We look at war as though it were something absolutely independent of the will of those who take part in it. And consequently we do not even admit the natural question, which presents itself to every simple person: "How about me — ought I to take any part in it?" No question of this kind even exists for us, and therefore every person, however he may regard war from a personal standpoint, slavishly submits to the requirements of the authorities on the subject.

•

Increase the military, then increase the tyranny — both at home and abroad.

•

Universal military service may be compared to the efforts of a man to prop up his falling house with props and buttresses and planks and scaffolding. He manages to keep the house standing but makes it impossible to live in it. Similarly, universal military service destroys all the benefits of the social order of life that it is employed to maintain. The taxes for war preparations absorb the greater part of the produce of labor, which the military is supposed to defend. The removal of men from the ordinary course of life undermines the need for productive labor. Finally, the danger of war, ever ready to break out, renders all reforms of social life vain and fruitless.

•

If two men get drunk in an inn and fight over cards I wouldn't venture to condemn only one of them. However convincing the arguments of the other may be, the cause of their ugly behavior isn't because one of them is right, but because instead of working peacefully they found it necessary to get drunk while playing cards in an inn.

Similarly, when people tell me that one side is solely to blame in a war that flares up, I can never agree. It may be the case that one side acts worse, but this doesn't explain even the immediate causes, let alone the origin, of the terrible, cruel, and inhuman phenomenon of war. To any person who doesn't shut his eyes to them, these causes are perfectly obvious.

•

It is those who do the beating, the handcuffing, the imprisoning, and the killing with their own hands that engage in violence. If there were no soldiers or armed policemen, however, ready to kill or outrage anyone as they are ordered, not one of those people who sign sentences of death, imprisonment, or galley-slavery for life would make up his mind to hang, imprison, or torture a fraction of those whom, quietly sitting in his study, he now orders to be tortured in all kinds of ways, simply because he does not see it nor do it himself, but only gets it done at a distance by these servile tools.

•

"How terrible," people say, "is war, with its wounds, bloodshed, and deaths. We must organize a Red Cross Society to alleviate the wounds, sufferings, and pains of death." But truly what is dreadful in war are not the wounds, sufferings, and deaths. The human race has always suffered these things. It is not suffering and death that are terrible, but that which allows people to inflict suffering and death. It is not the suffering and mutilation and death of one's body that most needs to be diminished — it is the mutilation and death of one's soul. What is needed is not the Red Cross but the simple cross of Christ.

•

If someone has a drinking problem and I tell him that it is he who has to decide whether to stop drinking or not, then there is some hope that he will listen to me. But if I tell him that his problem is a complicated and difficult one that only the experts can solve, then in all probability he will continue to drink.

So it is with all the false and refined strategies to end war, such as international courts, arbitration, and similar absurdities with which we moderns occupy ourselves. For in all these approaches, the most simple, essential, and self-evident solution to ending war is carefully omitted.

The way to do away with war is for those who do not want war, and who are morally bothered about all that makes for war, to refrain from fighting. This is what the earliest Christians did, and many others, like the Quakers, have followed suit.

GOVERNMENT

When, among a hundred people one person dominates ninety-nine, it is iniquity, it is despotism; when ten dominate ninety, it is injustice, it is oligarchy; when fifty-one dominate forty-nine (and this only theoretically, for in reality, among these fifty-one there are ten or eleven who control things), then it is justice, then it is liberty.

•

Government is an association of men who do violence to the rest of us.

•

How can justice have any binding force on a ruler or rulers who keep the people deluded and drilled in readiness for acts of violence?

•

In all history there is no war that was not hatched by the governments, the governments alone, independent of the interests of the people, to whom war is always pernicious even when successful.

•

The words "Christian state" resemble the words "hot ice." Such an entity is either not a state, or it is not Christian.

•

True Christianity puts an end to government. For this reason, Christ was crucified. Only from the time that the heads of government assumed the semblance of Christianity did people devise ways by which Christianity could be reconciled with government. But no honest and serious-minded person can help seeing the incompatibility of Christ — his teaching of meekness, forgiveness of injuries, and love — with government, with its pomp, acts of violence, executions, and wars.

TO LOVE

Love is the essential faculty of the human soul. We love not because it is our interest to do so but because love is the essence of who we are, because we cannot but love.

•

A horse is not unhappy when it cannot crow like a rooster but only when it loses what is natural to it — its swift flight. It is not sad when people die, lose their money, or do not have a home or property — none of this intrinsically belongs to people. It is sad when people lose what really belongs to them and is their greatest happiness — their ability to love.

•

We are created for love: to love and to be loved. For this reason we cannot force ourselves to be loving. No matter how you shake or turn a corked bottle, nothing will flow until you take out the cork. The same goes for love. Your soul is actually full of love; but that love will not come out until your sin is removed. Get rid of what clogs your soul, and you will love.

•

Love of your neighbor without love of God is a plant without roots.

•

Everything that I understand, I understand only because I love. Everything exists, only because I love. Everything is united by it alone. Love is God, and to die means that I, a particle of love, shall return to the general and eternal source.

•

If "I" am "I," the same "I" as sixty or thirty years ago, or two hours ago, it is because I love this "I"; because love binds these separate "I"s, these "I"s that are spread out over time into one whole. With regard to time I can clearly see how love binds together these different "I"s and gathers them into one.

With regard to space the same thing happens in my body. A physiologist would say that my hand is "mine" because I am one organism and my nerves inform me of this unity through pain. But why do I feel pain? It is because I love everything that makes up my body. Love has knitted it together.

Dickens writes of an amputee who carries his leg around in a bottle and loves it. A mother loves the locks of hair cut from her child, and feels pain when they are destroyed. In the same way one can love people who live before, people who are ill, and their sufferings. Love for one's "I" within certain limits of space and time is what we call life. Our life is the fruit of the preceding sphere of love, while our future life will depend on the extent of our sphere of love in this life.

•

It is love that makes us see beauty, not beauty.

•

The very best love is unconscious love.

•

It is a mistake to think that there are times when you can safely relate to a person without love. You can work with objects without love — cutting wood, baking bricks, making iron — but you cannot be with people without love. As you cannot work with bees without being cautious, you also cannot work with people without being mindful of their humanity. As with bees, if you are not cautious with others, then you harm both yourself and them.

•

People learn to fly, but don't learn to love. It is as if birds were to stop flying and learn to ride bicycles instead.

•

Just as all the water drains out of a bucket with even the tiniest hole, all the joy of life drains from our soul when we hate even one person.

•

If you wish to correct your neighbor, tell him simply what he did wrong. If he does not listen to you, do not blame him but blame yourself for not having figured out how to tell him the best way. Asking how many times you should forgive your neighbor is like asking a person who decides not to drink how many times he should refuse wine when it is offered to him. If I decide not to drink, then I won't drink, no matter how many times it is offered to me. The same applies to forgiveness.

•

If you are in a difficult situation, or in a low mood, if you are afraid of other people and of yourself, if you are tormented, then tell yourself, "I will love everyone whom I meet in this life." Try to follow this rule; and you will see that everything will find its way, and everything will seem simple, and you will no longer have doubts or fears.

UNITY AND FRATERNITY

A river does not look like a pond; a pond does not look like a puddle; a puddle does not look like a cup of water. But the water in the river, the pond, the puddle, and the cup is the same. It is the same with people — people are different but the spirit living in them is the same.

•

God makes all people equal. He takes from those who have much and gives to those who have little. The rich man has more things but less joy from them. The poor person has fewer things but more joy from them. Water from a stream and a crust of bread taste far better to a poor laborer than the most expensive food and drink taste to a spoiled, idle person. The rich overeat, are bored, and do not get any lasting pleasure from anything. The enjoyment of a person who works hard is renewed every time he has a meal, a drink, or some rest.

•

Christ proclaimed equality, not on the basis of our relation
to the Infinite, but in our relation to the Father as his sons.
Anything other than this message is a deception.

•

Why do we feel bad when we disagree with someone and feel
still worse when we are angry at him? Because whatever is in
us that makes us human beings is the same in everyone. So,
when we do not love people, we are disconnecting ourselves
from what is the same in everyone; in other words, we are
disconnecting ourselves from ourselves.

•

If two people are going from Moscow to Kiev — it does not
matter how far apart they are, say, one is just about to enter
Kiev and one has just left Moscow — they are both going to the
same place and sooner or later will meet each other. By contrast, no matter how close two people are, if one is going to
Kiev and the other to Moscow, they will always be apart. It is
the same with people. A godly person who lives for his soul
and the worst sinner who nevertheless also lives for his soul are
both on the same path and will both meet sooner or later. If
two people are living together, but one lives for himself and his
pleasures and the other lives for others and his soul, they cannot
help drifting further and further apart.

•

I can be close to my family, but what about others? I can be
close to my friends, to my fellow countrymen, but what about
people I do not know and who are unlike me? Other eth-
nic groups? People of different faiths? How can I be close to
these? There is only one way — forget about people and do not
think about getting close to them but instead think about how
to come close to the one Spiritual Being who lives in me and
everyone else.

•

We can unite with each other only in God. We do not need to take steps toward each other; we need only to approach God. If there were a huge church in which the light from above fell only in the center, people would only have to go toward the light in the center to be gathered together. Be assured, if we all approach God, we will be drawn toward each other.

LIVING JUSTLY

As long as I have food I don't need when someone else has none, or have two coats and someone else has none, I share in a constantly repeated crime.

•

The worst thief is not the one who takes what he needs but the one who keeps what he does not need when others need it.

•

It is tempting to think, especially for those who live in countries of relative freedom and where there exists the semblance of educational and economic opportunity, that by working hard we are doing our part — at least we are not destroying the lives of others. Isn't prosperity the legitimate reward of hard work? Somehow we forget about the thousands working in the mines for the sake of our obsession with glittering trinkets. We forget, not seeing them, those in distant lands who barely survive, working for our caprices. The link between our luxury and the privations of millions is the price paid outright in human life, whereby our comforts and luxury are purchased.

•

It would be very strange for a shoemaker to think that people were bound to feed him because, indeed, he continued to make shoes nobody wanted. What then shall we say about all those in government, church, education, science, and art who not only do not produce anything tangibly useful, but whose "product" nobody really wants or needs?

•

In seeking to heal our social diseases we look everywhere — to the government, anti-government, scientific and philanthropic ideals — and yet we do not see that which meets the eyes of everyone. We fill our drains with filth, and require others to clean them, and pretend to feel very sorry for them, and we want to ease their work, and invent all kinds of devices except one, the simplest; namely, that we should ourselves remove our garbage so long as we find it necessary to produce waste in our homes.

•

When you feed hens and chickens, if the old hens and cocks make trouble — if they pick up the food more quickly and drive off the weak ones — it's not likely that by giving them more food the hungry ones can be satisfied. You have to imagine in this case that the cocks and hens that drive the others off are insatiable. Since you can't kill the cocks and hens that drive the others off, it's all a question of teaching them to share with the weak ones. Until this happens, there will always be famine.

•

The gap between our life and the Christian ideal is so enormous, it is so far from what it ought to be, that to succeed in Christ's revolution, for the concordance of conscience and life, the work of all people is needed — people living in communities as well as people of the world living in the most dire conditions. Only when every person in the whole world can say, "Why should I sell my services and buy yours? If mine are greater than yours I owe them to you," only then will Christ's revolution succeed. We cannot be saved separately, we must be saved all together. Let us remember that we are messengers representing the great King — the God of Love with the message of unity and love between all living beings.

PROPERTY AND POSSESSIONS

Wealth should be like manure in the field. When it is in a big pile it makes a bad smell. But when it is distributed everywhere across the field, it makes the soil fertile.

•

Now that people are "free," I can compel Ivan and Peter and Sidor to do every kind of work with impunity. If they refuse to do it, I withhold paying them money — money they will need to pay taxes. They will be punished until they too submit. If they refuse to work exactly as I wish, they will go without money, and in turn will go without bread.

Books on political economy persuade me that in a money economy all people are free. But our peasants have long known that with a ruble one can hurt more than with a stick. To say that money does not create bondage is like saying that the servitude of a century and a half ago did not create slavery. Common wisdom says that money is an inoffensive medium of exchange, notwithstanding the fact that, in consequence of possessing it, one person may practically enslave another.

•

A certain rich man had everything — millions of dollars, a gorgeous estate, a beautiful wife, hundreds of employees, sumptuous meals, snacks, wines, and a stable full of expensive horses. He was so tired of all this that he sat in his bedroom all day long, sighing and complaining of boredom.

The only thing that still brought him any pleasure was eating. Upon waking, he looked forward to breakfast. After breakfast, he look forward to lunch; after lunch, to dinner. But it was not long before he was deprived of even this satisfaction. He ate so much good food that he ruined his stomach and could not enjoy his meals. He called the doctors. The doctors prescribed medicine and told him to walk two hours a day.

One day a poor person approached him as he was walking his prescribed two hours. He was thinking about his plight, and particularly about his lack of appetite. The poor person begged, "Please, for the love of Christ, give me some money." But the rich man was so absorbed in thinking about the misery of not being able to eat he did not hear the poor person's plea.

"Please, sir, I have not eaten all day." These words about eating penetrated the rich man's thoughts and he stopped. "You want to eat?" "How could I not, sir, I am very hungry. I am only a poor peasant." The rich man thought, "Such a lucky man he is," and envied the poor man.

The poor envy the rich, and the rich envy the poor. In the end, everyone is on equal footing. Only the poor are better off, because they usually do not bear any guilt for being poor; but the rich are always guilty of being wealthy as long as there are the poor.

SUFFERING AND DEATH

We can respond in one of two ways toward suffering: either we see suffering as something to endure, something pointless, a torture devoid of meaning, or we can embrace the fact that my sin, in one way or another, is the cause of my suffering, and that my suffering is there to release and redeem me from sin. According to the one, suffering should not exist. It has no explanation. To the other, suffering must be, for it has inward significance for my life.

●

Wherein lies true suffering? Suffering consists of being conscious of my sinfulness and how my sin contradicts life and then to feel further how far I am from realizing in my own person the truth which seeks to manifest itself in the world.

●

If you are not strong, ask for troubles to make you so.

•

Your illness will disappear, not as a result of treatment or doctors or even the climate, but because the time will come for it to disappear, as with all illnesses which eventually disappear. If you have to undergo treatment, then choose what is simpler, less worrisome and expensive, and less preoccupying. All health resorts, for example, have this failing: everybody in them is occupied with his own ailments, and one can't help learning to ascribe to health or ill-health more importance than it deserves.

•

If we grumble at sickness, God won't grant us death.

•

Suffering is not an evil that you must be rid of, but the work of your life that you must accept. In wishing to evade your suffering, you resemble a man who fails to push the plow where the ground is hardest.

•

Without suffering we know neither our limitations, nor ourselves.

•

One thing I can say is that my own illness has helped me. A great deal of nonsense vanished when I faced up in earnest to God. I came to see how much was rotten in me that I hadn't seen before. And I began to feel a bit easier. Perhaps, then, we ought to say to people we love: I don't want you to be well, I want you to be ill.

•

If the gods had created us without the ability to experience pain, we would very soon begin to beg for it.

•

The questions, "Why?" and "To what purpose?" in the face of suffering only show that we have not recognized what it is that frees suffering from its torture.

•

There may be less charm in life when we think of death, but there's more peace.

•

Why do children die? I could never find an answer, not until I began thinking of my own life and human life in general. I am now convinced that our only task is to increase the love within us, and by increasing this love to infect others with it and increase the love within them. Why did this little boy live and die without having lived through a tenth part of a normal person's life? The answer is that he lived to increase love, to grow in love, since this was required by the One who sent him, and to infect all of us around him with this same love, so that when departing this life to join Him who is love, he could leave behind in us the love that had grown in him and unite us with it. [In reference to Tolstoy's youngest son, Ivan, who died a month before his seventh birthday.]

ETERNAL LIFE

You are afraid of death, but ask yourself what it would be like if you had to live forever as the person you are now.

•

If I were to write about the events in my life, there are few of them and they don't interest me. But if I were to write about my inner life, what I've been thinking about, it's an inexhaustible subject. The main thing is that I am preparing for death, i.e., for another life, and this preparation consists entirely in living as well as possible and trying to understand what can be understood. I believe that all this will be useful *there*, as it is here.

•

Death is the transformation of the envelope that contains our spirit. Do not confuse the envelope with its contents.

•

The confines of our body give form to the divine spirit the same way a vessel gives form to the liquid or gas it contains. When the vessel breaks, its contents no longer take the same form but spill out. Do they unite with other elements? Do they receive a new form? We do not know, but we do know the contents lose the form they had while confined, because "that which contained it" was destroyed. We know this, but we cannot know anything about what happens to "that which was confined." We only know that after death the soul becomes something different, and we are not able to form any conclusions about it in this life.

MISCELLANIES

Our good qualities do us far more harm than our bad ones.

•

Asking God to give us happiness is like asking God to quench our thirst when we are sitting next to a spring. Bend over and take a drink.

•

There is no middle way: you are a slave either of people or of God.

•

Those people speak most who do not have much to say.

•

Either be silent or say things that are worth more than silence.

•

One of the most dangerous temptations is the temptation to prepare to live, instead of living.

•

Christ did not tell us to love one another, but preached repentance, *metanoia*, that is to say, a change of thinking regarding life itself: change your whole conception of life, he said, or you will perish.

•

We dislike people not because they are evil; we think they are evil because we dislike them.

•

To keep ourselves totally apart so as not to become sullied is the most sullied thing of all.

•

Iron is more solid than stone; stone is more solid than wood; wood is more solid than water; water is more solid than air. But there is something that we cannot feel, see, or hear that is more solid than everything else. It is the only thing that was, is, will be, and never will disappear. What is it? The human soul!

•

From a five-year-old boy to me is only a step, from a newborn babe to a five-year-old boy there is an immense distance, from an embryo to a newborn babe there is an enormous chasm, while between nonexistence and an embryo there is not merely a chasm but incomprehensibility.

•

Remorse is like the cracking of an eggshell or a grain of corn, as a result of which the seed starts to grow.

•

Humankind survives earthquakes, epidemics, terrible diseases, and every kind of spiritual suffering, but always the most poignant tragedy was, is, and ever will be the tragedy of the bedroom.

•

It is good that I am ashamed of myself, but I must not take pride in this fact.

•

We might compare our society to a house built, not even on sand, but on ice. Its foundation is melting, and the house is beginning to fall in.

•

People are always astonished that in the developed nations every year there are thousands of suicides. We ought rather to be surprised that there are so few.

•

Apart from death there is no single act so important, clear-cut, all-transforming, and irreversible as marriage.

•

What counts in making a happy marriage is not so much how compatible you are, but how you deal with incompatibility.

•

We are not a lake but a river, and furthermore, a river that dries up in places, as in the steppes. The river is sometimes broad, sometimes deep, sometimes shallow. Sometimes it is only mud, sometimes it is dirty, sometimes clean, sometimes fast, sometimes still; but it is always the same river. So it is with us. Sometimes we are near to Christ, sometimes to a swine. Once we realize this it is easier to move in the direction of Christ and away from the swine. But if I imagine that I am a good Christian, I will never understand where my life ends and the swine begins. There is a Christian teaching and a Christian ideal, but there is not, and cannot be, a Christian.

•

We can only really understand ourselves when we can see ourselves in everyone else.

•

A million times more harm has probably been done and is being done by love of work than by idleness. Lao-tzu derives all the evil in the world directly from people's concern for their own and other people's apparent good. And however strange it is, one can't help but agreeing with him. Famines are the result of our being too concerned about feeding — we have plowed everything up; our illness the result of our worrying too much about health — hence our state of enervation; the insecurity and danger of our lives the result of worrying too much about safety — hence our governments, police forces, armies. The reason for our slavery is that we worry about freedom — hence our obligations to take part in governing. The reason for our ignorance is that we worry about enlightenment — hence all the preaching in our churches.

•

During a performance someone thought it would be funny to yell "Fire." Everyone tried to run out the doors. They all pushed and shoved and when things had finally calmed down, twenty people had been trampled to death and fifty injured. This is the kind of evil that one word can do. But often more harm is done by the stupid word that is not so immediately evident. It does its insidious work imperceptibly, bit by bit.

•

We torture ourselves with the past and in our worry spoil the future simply because we do not pay sufficient attention to the present. The past is gone. The future does not exist. There is only now.

•

If you recall a long conversation and really review what was said, you will be amazed at how empty, unnecessary, and even malicious most of it was.

•

If a bird runs on its legs, it does not prove that it is not its nature to fly. If we see around us people who make their aim their own happiness, this does not prove that we are not capable of living beyond ourselves.

•

A man is like a fraction whose numerator is what he is and whose denominator is what he thinks of himself. The larger the denominator the smaller the fraction.

•

In this life we are like stubborn horses put into harnesses and shafts. At first, we kick. We want to live according to our will. We break the shafts, snap the harness, do not go anywhere, and become exhausted. Finally when we are at the end and we are not thinking about getting our own way anymore, we give in to the Higher Will, and things move forward. This is when we find peace and happiness.

•

If you wish to better your life, be ready to sacrifice it.

Sources

The selections in this volume come from numerous English collections and editions of Tolstoy's works. In a majority of cases, the editor has taken the liberty to rework translations by abridging lengthy pieces, paraphrasing complex or wordy passages, and tightening and simplifying sentence construction. Since the collected works of Tolstoy are not readily available, the editor has made reference to separate editions after each selection.

Tolstoy's Life

Carroll, Sara Newton. *The Search: A Biography of Leo Tolstoy.* New York: Harper and Row, 1973.

Collis, John Stewart. *Leo Tolstoy.* London: House of Stratus, 2001.

Crankshaw, Edward. *Tolstoy: The Making of a Novelist.* New York: Viking Press, 1974.

Crosby, Ernest Howard. *Tolstoy and His Message.* New York: Funk & Wagnall, 1904.

Maude, Aylmer. *Leo Tolstoy and His Work.* London: Routledge & Sons, 1930.

Tolstoy, Leo. *Childhood, Boyhood, Youth.* New York: Scribner, 1904.

———. *The Diaries of Leo Tolstoy.* New York: E. P. Dutton, 1917.

Tolstoy, Sonya. *Diary of Tolstoy's Wife, 1860–1891.* London: Payson and Clark, 1929.

Tolstoy, Tatyana. *Tolstoy Remembered.* New York: McGraw-Hill, 1977.

Troyat, Henri. *Tolstoy.* New York: Doubleday, 1967.

Wilson, A. N. *Tolstoy.* New York: Norton, 1988.

Zweig, Stefan. *The Living Thoughts of Tolstoy.* Philadelphia: David McKay, 1939.

Collected Works in English

The Complete Works of Count Tolstoy. 24 vols. Trans. Leo Wiener. Boston: Dana Estes and Company, 1904.

The Works of Leo Tolstoy. Centenary Edition. 21 vols. Trans. Louise Maude and Aylmer Maude. London: Oxford University Press, 1929.

Tolstoy's Religious Writings (separate editions)

A Calendar of Wisdom. Trans. Peter Sekirin. New York: Scribner, 1997.

Christianity and Patriotism. Trans. Constance Garnett. London: J. Cape, 1922.

A Confession, The Gospel in Brief, and What I Believe. London: Oxford University Press, 1974.

Essays and Letters. Trans. Aylmer Maude. London: Oxford University Press, 1911.

Essays, Letters, Miscellanies. New York: Thomas Y. Crowell, 1899.

The Kingdom of God Is within You. Lincoln: University of Nebraska Press, 1984.

The Law of Love and the Law of Violence. New York: Holt, Rinehart and Winston, 1970.

Leo Tolstoy: Selected Essays. Selected and introduced by Ernest J. Simmons. New York: Random House, 1964.

Lift up Your Eyes: The Religious Writings of Leo Tolstoy. Introduction by Stanley R. Hopper. New York: Julian Press, 1960.

On Life and Essays on Religion. Trans. Aylmer Maude. London: Oxford University Press, 1934.

The Religious Writings of Tolstoy (The Lion and the Honeycomb). Ed. A. N. Wilson. Trans. Robert Chandler. London: William Collins, 1987.

The Sayings of Leo Tolstoy. Ed. Robert Pearce. London: Duckworth, 2003.

Tolstoy's Diaries. 2 vols. Ed. and trans. R. F. Christian. New York: HarperCollins, 1996.

Tolstoy's Letters. 2 vols. Ed. and trans. R. F. Christian. New York: Charles Scribner's Sons, 1978.

What Is to Be Done? New York: Charles Scribner's Sons, 1904.

The Wisdom of Tolstoy. New York: Citadel Press, 1968.

Writings on Civil Disobedience and Nonviolence. Philadelphia: New Society Publishers, 1987.